Fold Forming
for Jewellers *and*
Metalsmiths

Fold Forming
for Jewellers *and*
Metalsmiths

Louise Mary Muttitt

THE CROWOOD PRESS

First published in 2017 by
The Crowood Press Ltd
Ramsbury, Marlborough
Wiltshire SN8 2HR

www.crowood.com

British Library Cataloguing-in-Publication Data
A catalogue record for this book is available from the British Library.

ISBN 978 1 78500 272 4

Frontispiece: *Leaf Bowl and Scoop* by Louise Mary Muttitt

Dedication
To my children, my rays of sunshine, Bryony and Freddy

Typeset by Kelly-Anne Levey
Printed and bound in India by Replika Press Pvt Ltd

CONTENTS

INTRODUCTION

What is Fold Forming?

Fold forming is the name coined by Canadian metalsmith Charles Lewton-Brain to describe the process of folding sheet metal, then somehow compressing the fold usually with a hammer. This folded piece is then sometimes further worked into by forging, before opening out to reveal the created form. Charles Lewton-Brain is the inventor and the world leader in developing the science and art known as fold forming, and there are now many artists and metalsmiths around the world exploring this fascinating technique.

When fold forming is carried out on a piece of sheet metal, it is distorted and shaped in ways that result in the maker having a greater understanding of the properties of sheet metal. Some amazing forms are created that very strongly imitate those found in nature. It is as if the forms have 'grown' from the metal, which is a good way to think of the process when practising it.

When forging the metal during fold forming the metal becomes thinner, but this does not necessarily weaken the form; in fact the resulting fold makes it stronger structurally. Fold forming is a very free process, and the maker can make

Fig. 0.1 A collection of fold forms by the inventor of fold forming, Charles Lewton-Brain.

decisions about the form being created while working on it in an intuitive manner. As it is a less restrictive process than some other metalworking methods, it enables artists to express their ideas through form in a dynamic way.

Among the many different influences on fold forming are the crafts of origami and textiles, for example paper chains and smocking. However, metal can go much further than paper or fabric. The properties of metal allow it to be manipulated and stretched thin like clay yet hold its shape like card. From even the simplest of folding techniques, there is great joy to be found in discovering and exploring the processes described in this book, and from these many starting points you can go on to explore and discover on your own. Chapter 5 gives some pointers for this onward journey.

Discovering Fold Forming

For me, discovering fold forming was serendipitous. I initially had no idea that the process I was exploring was already a named technique, and so my early work evolved on a trial and error basis. It came about during my university degree at Sheffield Hallam University. In 2005 I was working on my final year project, creating spoons. I initially tried the traditional technique of forging the spoon from a bar of metal. The main reason that spoons are forged in this way is so that the main bowl of the spoon is forged from a thicker piece of metal in order to retain thickness at the weakest point in the spoon, which is where the handle meets the bowl. When trying this technique, I realized this was a very time-consuming and labour-intensive

Fig. 0.2 Fold-formed leaf spoons in sterling silver by Louise Mary Muttitt.

Fig. 0.3 Traditional silversmithing techniques can be incorporated into fold formed pieces. Here, the technique of blocking using a wooden egg-shaped mallet supported on a leather sandbag is being used to add a soft curve to the form of a silver leaf bowl that has already had a line fold worked into the sheet metal.

process, so I wondered if there was a way to create this strength at the point where the handle meets the bowl using another method. At the same time as considering this practical problem, my workspace was covered in gathered visual research, consisting mainly of structures from nature that combine elegance and delicacy with engineered brilliance; this visual research spanned diverse forms from seed heads to feathers and leaves.

With these in mind, I began working from sheet metal and creating leaf shapes with long stems, imagining the leaf as the bowl of the spoon and the stem as the handle. I then managed to make use of an industrial metalworking tool in the university workshop, through which I could pass the metal to create a bend. My leaf spoons now had a spine, which made them strong along their entire length. I had found a solution and it was considerably less labour-intensive than the traditional forging method: no soldering required, and strength naturally running along the handle into the bowl of the spoon. There was also the surprising additional benefit of this shape being very ergonomic.

When I left university in 2005 I no longer had access to the industrial bending tool so I had to work out how to make my leaf spoons with the limited tools I had available. I began folding the metal freehand using a hide mallet and a vice, then passing the folded metal through the rolling mill, annealing and opening the fold formed spoon. The process was a success, and in the years since I have

Fig. 0.4 The author at work in her studio in South Derbyshire.

continued experimenting and refining these techniques based on a trial and error approach to develop my range of silverware and jewellery, incorporating my own version of fold forming. The range now includes pieces of silverware such as candlesticks and vases, and many pieces of jewellery such as earrings, bracelets and neck-laces. Subtle variations in metal thickness and scale are considered to ensure that my pieces are practical as well as aesthetically appealing, and the strong influence of natural forms is still highly evident in my work.

In 2012 I attended a summer school at Birmingham School of Jewellery taught by inspiring metalsmith Cynthia Eid. It was so interesting to be 'taught' the process which I had already explored extensively indepen-dently. As well as broadening my knowledge of basic fold forming, the course also intro-duced me to micro folding and use of Argen-tium silver, which lends itself very well to fold forming. Armed with even more tools and also having dedicated a full week to freely experi-menting – not something I can often do as a

Fig. 0.5 Basic metalsmithing hand skills are required to create fold formed designs. Here, filing a piece of silver wire supported on a bench peg, prior to incorporating this into a finished piece.

practising designer/maker – my fold-forming work has progressed further than I could have ever imagined from those first few experiments at university. Attending a course for a technique such as fold forming is very stimulating as the other course participants discover and experiment alongside you, sharing their discoveries and bringing their thoughts to the process. This experience is particularly rewarding for those of us who spend most of our time working solo in our studios.

This book assumes an understanding of basic metalworking techniques such as annealing, saw piercing and soldering. Many of the processes for fold forming can be created with relatively few tools, essentially hammers, a vice, a planishing block or anvil, heating equipment for annealing and some basic bench tools such as a pair of metal snips. A rolling mill is an excellent asset too. Micro folding requires investment in more specialist equipment, although it is also possible to try out some simple micro folding with paper corrugating tools or a tube wringer initially before making a larger investment.

Across all techniques I have included bench tips from my own experience, which I hope will help you to master these processes. But as with all new techniques, practice makes perfect and any mistakes will also help your understanding of the metal and the techniques. Accurate folds will make your pieces successful, as will finding ways to open up forms without distorting or cracking. The really rewarding part is when an individual uses his or her own design flair to translate the interesting forms created into wonderful sculptural, wearable or useful pieces.

TOOLS, WORKSPACE AND METALS

Fold forming can be carried out with relatively few tools, many of which are common pieces of equipment in a jewellery or metalsmithing studio. By contrast, metal corrugation requires specialist equipment and there are several choices available; the tool options for metal corrugation are explained in detail in Chapter 4.

Fold-forming Tools

Basic Tool List

This short list of tools forms the basic set of equipment you will need to create most of the folds and their variations in Chapters 2 and 3. Each of these categories of tools is explained in more detail below.

Hammers: a planishing hammer, a forging hammer and a soft mallet
Vice, bolted to a secure surface
Anvil or steel flat plate
Rolling mill
Soldering area with torch, tongs
Metal shears
Opening tools

Hammers

Metal hammers are made in different ways and this affects their quality. A drop forged hammer is the highest quality, the longest lasting and usually the more expensive of all of them. Because they are forged, the metal is denser so they polish up very well. Alternatively there are cast hammerheads, which are cheaper but can be porous and brittle. Specialist hammers do tend to be expensive but they last for many years. Adapting old drop forged hammers can be an economical way to create bespoke and good quality hammers customized to particular requirements.

Planishing Hammer

A planishing hammer has one flat and one slightly curved perfectly polished face. In fold forming, a planishing hammer is used to confirm folds. Using the slightly curved face when confirming

Fig. 1.1 **Planishing hammer with one flat face and one slightly domed face, both faces polished to a perfect mirror finish.**

Fig. 1.2 Hammers for forging. The bottom one is a creasing hammer, the top hammer is a customized vintage hammer.

Fig. 1.3 The cross pein of this hammer has been filed to a soft curve to make it perfect for forging along an edge in fold forming.

Fig. 1.4 A leather mallet and a nylon mallet. The nylon hammer has screw-on ends, which can be replaced when worn out.

folds is ideal as it is less likely to catch the edge of the hammer, which can leave an unwanted mark. Look after a planishing hammer by storing it carefully between uses, wrapped in a piece of old towel to protect the face from damage from other tools or rust. Maintain its perfect finish by polishing on a rotating polishing machine using a calico mop and Hyfin polishing compound. If deeper dents occur, remove these with a file and wet and dry paper, working through the grades to 400 before polishing with a calico mop and Hyfin.

Forging Hammer

A forging hammer has a long narrow pein, is heavy in weight and has a slightly curved profile; it also has a polished finish like the planishing hammer. The marks made by forging during fold forming are often left as a feature of the piece, so follow the advice for protecting and re-polishing the hammer face as above for the planishing hammer. When choosing the forging hammer for fold forming, make sure you select one with a broad enough face, as a hammer with a narrow face will only move the surface of the metal, whereas a broader face will move all the metal. To imagine this more clearly, think of the metal as a sheet of rolled out clay, being smoothed out with the ends of fingers as opposed to using something fine-pointed like a pencil tip, which would only make dents in the surface.

Commercially available raising hammers and creasing hammers can be used for forging in fold forming. It may be the case that you need to customize a hammer face, using a grinder or a file to create the perfect shape. Sourcing vintage hammers and changing their shape is an economical way to create a set of personalized hammers perfect for different jobs. My own favourite hammer is a vintage hammer which I re-shaped to create a perfect profile using a bench grinder. I have also modified my creasing hammer in a similar way by softening the corners to prevent the edges catching while forging. Consider the scale of the work when selecting a forging hammer: the finer and smaller the work, the smaller the forging hammer you will require.

Mallets

Mallets are made from softer materials – leather, wood and plastic – and are mostly used for flattening and smoothing sheet metal. All of these materials are useful for moving metal with very little stretching or marking. In practice, leather mallets are very efficient and have a reasonable weight to them. Mallets with interchangeable screw-in plastic heads are also very useful as the heads can be custom-shaped for specific jobs and can be replaced when worn out.

Fig. 1.5 A sturdy engineer's vice bolted securely to the corner of a wooden workbench, with plenty of room to move around so that the vice can be approached from different angles.

Vice

A vice is an essential piece of equipment for fold forming. Ensure it is bolted securely to the workbench and that there is plenty of space to move around it so you can approach the vice from a variety of angles. When installing a vice also make sure it is at a height that you can work at comfortably.

A fairly substantial vice with 10cm- (4"-) wide jaws is ideal for a wide variety of fold-forming techniques. If you go for a second-hand vice, check that the vice jaws are level.

A leg vice is a great asset if you have access to one, as the force of impact during forging is absorbed directly into the ground.

Anvil or Flat Plate

You will need a flat steel surface as a supporting surface when compressing and forging folds. It might be worth having an old flat plate or anvil which can be used for copper experiments, and a clean, smooth flat plate to use when working in

precious metals or when looking to create very clean, neat folds with a planishing hammer. When starting out at fold forming, depending on your level of experience with forging, it can be easy to slip and mark the flat plate, so an old flat plate is ideal when practising. A rounded or chamfered edge to the flat plate is also useful, as forging during fold forming is usually done working along the edge of the flat plate and so a softer edge helps to prevent marks forming from underneath.

Rolling Mill

As with the vice, a rolling mill must be securely bolted down and you should have easy access to it from both sides. When selecting a rolling mill, choose the widest mill possible to enable larger scale forms to be created. A rolling mill with a measurement guide on the top is very useful as it can be set to specific sizes accurately; keep a record of these as you are working as a useful reference when developing your designs.

Fig. 1.6 **Rolling mill securely bolted to a purpose-built cupboard. This also needs plenty of space around it to pass metal through and to turn the handle.**

Fig. 1.7 **Soldering hearth lined with fire-proof bricks.**

Soldering Area

Metal needs to be annealed frequently during fold forming, so a hearth or similar area needs to be set up for this purpose. Second-hand hearths can be found easily, otherwise build one from suitable materials which are able to withstand the heat from the flame.

Select a torch that will heat the metal to annealing temperature; for most metals such as copper this is when the metal starts to glow a dark cherry red. A Sievert torch is an ideal choice for many metalsmiths. A pair of tongs or tweezers will also be required to pick up the hot metal.

To remove the oxides from the surface of the metal after annealing, use a specialist acid solution such as Safety Pickle gently warmed in a pickle tank or slow cooker. A pair of brass or plastic tweezers or tongs are required to take metals in and out of the pickle. After pickling, clean the metal by scrubbing with an old toothbrush using pumice powder, warm water and a little washing-up liquid.

Metal Shears

Metal shears or snips are required for cutting the open edge of folded forms during fold forming. A piercing saw can be used to shape metal prior to fold forming but as this creates fine metal dust which can work inside the fold, resulting in a pitted surface after forging, snips are often a better option when cutting folded forms.

Opening Tools

One of the trickiest aspects of fold forming can be opening the folded form after hammering or rolling. Using a tool that can be inserted into the open edge of the metal without marking is a great advantage. Depending on the scale and depth of the fold to be opened, a range of opening tools might be required. These suggested tools include re-purposed commercial tools and tools I have made myself.

Re-Purposed Commercial Tools
Straight burnisher
Watch-back opener
Plastic clay-modelling tools

Handmade Tools
Wooden and plastic offcuts cut into wedge
shapes
Fine-tipped opening tool for small work carved
from a hard plastic toothbrush handle (the
brush itself is useful for cleaning out the corrugated rolling mill, *see* Chapter 4)

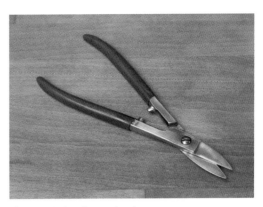

Fig. 1.8 Pair of metal snips.

Additional Tools

These additional tools are either used for a
few specialist fold-forming techniques or are
non-essential but help to make part of the fold-
forming process easier.

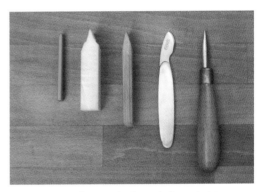

Fig. 1.9 Opening tools, from left to right:
handmade tool from toothbrush handle,
handmade tool from a piece of nylon,
handmade tool from a piece of wood,
watch-back opening tool, straight burnisher.

Vice Jaws

Most vice jaws are rough and some are not quite
level. These problems can be overcome by protecting the vice jaws with a pair of magnetic
rubber vice jaws. Magnetic rubber vice jaws are
inexpensive, can be applied quickly, stay firmly in
place and the rubber does not mark the metal.
However, as they are too soft to forge onto, for
creating multiple folds such as T-folds it is possible
to make simple vice jaws from sheet copper; these
will also protect the work from being marked.

Soldering Equipment

Soldering equipment is only required for a
few fold techniques, as one of the benefits of
fold forming is that amazing forms are created

Fig. 1.10 Magnetic rubber and aluminium vice
jaws for protecting metal from being marked
while held in the vice.

without soldering. If needing to solder, then a suitable flux and brush to apply the flux as well as the relevant solder (dependent on the metal being soldered) will be required.

Nylon Pliers, Flat and Round

Nylon pliers have become an indispensable workshop tool for manipulating metal sheet or wire without marking, and have many uses beyond fold forming. Many come with replaceable jaws as they do get marked and worn with use.

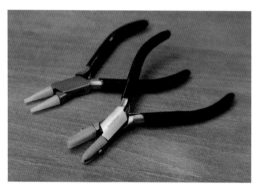

Fig. 1.11 Round-nosed and flat-nosed nylon pliers – replacement tips are available as these do wear out over a period of use.

Fig. 1.12 Chasing punches, doming punches and chasing hammer for repoussé work.

Binding Wire and Masking Tape

Binding wire and masking tape are required for curved folds in Chapter 2.

Pendant Motor Fitted with a Cutting Disc

A pendant motor fitted with a cutting disc is used to create quick scored curved folds in Chapter 2.

Chasing Hammer, Chasing Punches and Doming Punches

These tools are required for repoussé work on fold-formed pieces.

Workspace

A Safe Working Environment

It is very important to consider your health and safety when working with metal. This book assumes the reader is familiar with metalworking techniques and therefore also their relative appropriate safety precautions, but here is a brief outline of the basics.

Set up a well-ordered, secure workspace. Look after tools by keeping them stored tidily in a dry cupboard or similar when not in use. Ensure that equipment is set up at sensible heights for working to prevent back and eye strain. While working in your studio, try to get into the habit of keeping your workspace tidy and not leaving items lying around that could be trip hazards, or obstructions such as tools sticking out of a vice which could cause injury. Brush down your workbench daily and gather precious metal dust for recycling. Store any chemicals in glass or ceramic bottles, preferably in a locked cupboard, and make sure that they are clearly labelled. Safety data sheets are available from tools suppliers for chemicals and other items such as borax and polishes; please refer to these for specific health and safety advice as applicable. Dispose of chemicals responsibly, and neutralize acids with soda ash. Keep water away from tools as this can cause them to rust.

When working, wear sensible, enclosed flat shoes, tie up long hair, remove scarves and long jewellery items, and tuck in any loose clothing which could potentially get caught while working. Metalsmithing is not the cleanest enterprise, so it is probably wise to avoid wearing the finest items from your wardrobe, too. At times, jewellery making can be so absorbing that time seems to fly, but even if you are under time pressure to get work finished, take regular breaks.

Protective Wear

As standard practice in a metalsmithing studio, the following protective gear should be available to wear.

Apron

Always wear an apron, and make sure it is made of substantial material. Leather aprons are a good option, but at the very least select a robust kitchen apron made of a heavy weave fabric.

Pickle is a weak acid and will make holes in your clothes. An apron also provides an extra barrier if you drop sharp or hot objects.

Safety Glasses

These are essential for any jobs involving a rotating motor, such as drilling and polishing. Never undertake these tasks without goggles.

Rubber Gloves

These must be worn to protect your skin when using chemicals, for example when patinating silver.

Dust Mask (disposable)

These should be worn to protect your lungs from particle inhalation when sanding or polishing metal. Replace frequently.

First Aid Kit

It is a good idea to have a workshop first aid kit. This should include plasters, dressings, eyewash, antiseptic wipes and cream.

Fold-Forming Safety

The points below relate specifically to fold forming. As with all new techniques, take appropriate action to ensure that the environment and tools you are working with are safe. This includes but is not limited to checking tools are securely mounted onto the workbench, tightening the vice properly while working, checking the

Fig. 1.13 Kevlar gloves to protect hands, in particular when opening out fold-formed pieces as the thin edges can be very sharp.

hammerhead is not loose, and keeping fingers out of the way while hammering.

These are a few particular hazards of fold forming to be aware of:

Sharp Edges

The edges of the metal can become very thin and therefore sharp, so take care when handling and in particular opening out fold-formed pieces. Kevlar or similar gloves designed for metalworking are particularly useful for protecting fingers when doing this.

Noise

Most fold forming involves hammering. If doing a lot of hammering, ear protection in the form of earplugs or ear defenders should be worn to protect your hearing.

Repetitive Strain Injury

Repeated actions such as hammering can cause repetitive strain issues. Repetitive Strain Injury (RSI) is related to the overuse of muscles and tendons in the upper body. To avoid RSI, check your posture while working and adjust if necessary, take regular short breaks and try to avoid stress. Seek medical advice early if you think that you may be suffering from any of the symptoms of RSI, as prolonging working in the same activity can result in having to give up the activity altogether.

A Creative Workspace

With the safety aspects considered, it is important to mention that working in a positive environment and well laid-out studio can greatly enhance the creativity of metalsmithing. Lighting is key, and if natural daylight is available this is ideal. A light, bright space allows you to see your work clearly and helps avoid eye strain. For inspiration, use a

Fig. 1.14 A well organized, bright studio space to work in.

Fig. 1.15 The author's studio is an environment full of natural light, with an engineer's vice bolted onto a solid wooden worktop.

Fig. 1.16 A storage system that keeps tools tidy and close to hand on the workbench allows efficient working whilst keeping the working surface clear.

noticeboard to pin up sketches and imagery that inspire you and update it regularly as your work evolves.

Keep all your models, as these are a useful reference point when starting on new designs. Likewise, keep a record of what you have made, and any discoveries you have made during the process. This could include photographs or sketches, together with notes. These records will be invaluable as your fold-forming work develops.

Left: **Fig. 1.17 Assorted hammers are required for fold forming. Some can be customized from old engineer's hammers and some are purchased from specialist suppliers. Each metalsmith will build up a variety of hammers tailored to particular jobs over time.**

Fig. 1.18 Gathered visual research, models and sketches.

Fig. 1.19 Developing designs from copper experiments.

Metals

I recommend working in a base metal such as copper to make initial prototypes. Copper is an excellent metal to use for fold forming because it is soft, so responds well to being forged and can be pushed quite far between each round of annealing. It is also inexpensive for creating test pieces, allowing freedom to experiment.

Copper is not an ideal metal to use for final jewellery pieces that will come into direct contact with the body, as it tends to discolour the skin. Very few people are allergic to copper; this discolouration is just an oxide created from the mix of oils, sweat and the copper. Copper is a good metal for surface colouring, for example oxidizing or patinating green, and enamelling.

Once a design has been resolved in copper it can then be translated into precious metals to create jewellery or silverware designs. If working in sterling silver, be aware that it work-hardens more quickly than copper, making it more prone to cracking, therefore anneal more often. Britannia silver, Argentium silver and fine silver are all more ductile than sterling so are worth considering for creating finished pieces using fold forming. Please refer to Chapter 5 for further guidance on making metal choices for final pieces.

Figs 1.20 a,b,c The author sketching in her studio, reviewing copper fold formed experiments to create new designs.

SINGLE FOLDS

Single folds form the basis of fold forming. To learn how to fold form metal, begin by creating a single line fold in a sheet of metal. This starting point can be used to explore variations of flat folds, before moving onto forged folds, in which the folded or open edge is forged and therefore stretched, creating a dynamic three-dimensional form when the metal is opened after forging. These initial folds all create a straight fold on metal, and towards the end of this chapter two methods for creating curved folds are also introduced.

With some variations on the folds also included, these few techniques should open up a wealth of exploration opportunities. Many of the folds can be created quite rapidly, resulting in dramatic changes in the metal in just a few minutes.

Flat Line Fold

The most basic and quick fold to create is a flat line fold. If the metal is fully opened out after folding, it will leave a straight, raised line in a flat sheet of metal. It can be produced in a few minutes and is an ideal starting point. Trying this first will help you gain a basic understanding of the process before progressing onto more complex folds. The set of instructions below include some useful time-saving tips such as advice on quick cooling and cutting out, which are not repeated in as much depth in other processes

to save repetition, so please refer to this set of instructions as required when working through the procedures of other folds.

Basic Flat Line Fold

Tools & Materials

- 1 piece of soft sheet metal (copper is ideal), e.g. 40mm x 60mm, 0.3–0.5mm thick
- Basic tool kit
- Rolling mill (optional)

1. Anneal, pickle, rinse and dry the piece of sheet metal.

2. Using a marker pen and ruler, divide the sheet in half by marking a line down the centre of the sheet; ideally do this on both sides to aid accuracy.

Fig. 2.1 Marking out a line down the centre of the sheet metal using a steel ruler and fine marker pen.

3. Next, you need to bend the metal in half. With thin annealed copper sheet, you should find that you can do this with your fingers, bringing the two longest edges together as accurately as you can. For thicker or harder metals or narrow strips of metal, support in a vice, making sure to protect

Fig. 2.2 Tapping the metal in half using a mallet while the metal is gripped in a vice. The vice jaws are covered with magnetic rubber vice protectors to prevent the copper sheet from being marked by the vice jaws.

Fig. 2.3 Using the mallet to flatten the copper, which is now bent to a 90° angle.

Fig. 2.4 Bringing the two edges together to create the fold using the mallet, supported on a steel flat plate.

the metal from being marked by using vice jaws, with the marked line running parallel with the top of the vice jaws. Use a soft hammer such as a rubber or hide mallet to tap the metal into a 90° angle. Remove from the vice and support it on a smooth steel planishing block. Use the same mallet to close the fold; keep turning the metal over as you do this to create an even fold.

4. Still working on the steel planishing block, gently mallet the folded piece of metal flat, in preparation for compressing. Ensure you are still using a hide or rubber mallet at this stage; it is important not to use a metal hammer until the next stage.

5. Now you need to compress the fold – this creates the line that you will see when the sheet is opened out again. The more heavy-handed this is, the more defined the resulting fold will be. There are two options for compressing the fold. The first option is to planish the fold using the gently curved side of a metal planishing hammer with the piece of folded copper supported on a steel planishing block. Using the curved side of the hammer reduces the risk of catching the edge of the hammer and creating unsightly marks. Work evenly along the folded edge, making consistent steady blows with the hammer. The second option, which gives a very smooth, even and flat fold, is to pass the folded metal through a rolling mill. Set the rolling mill approximately two and a half times the thickness of

Fig. 2.5 Compressing the fold using a planishing hammer, supported on a steel flat plate.

Fig. 2.6 Compressing the fold by passing the folded metal through the rolling mill.

Fig. 2.7 Cutting around the open edge with a pair of metal snips.

Fig. 2.8 Opening the fold while supported in a vice after annealing by using a burnisher tapped gently with a mallet.

Fig. 2.9 Further opening out the fold using hands.

the initial sheet metal, so for example if using metal that is 0.5mm thick I would set the rolling mill to about 1.2mm for the first pass. I would then reduce it to 0.95mm, just under double the thickness of the original sheet, and pass the metal through a second time, resulting in a crisp and even fold.

6. At this point, with the metal still folded in half, you can cut the open edge of the metal to give a more interesting shape, which will be perfectly symmetrical once opened. If the metal is quite thin, use snips to cut at this stage, as using a piercing saw will create metal dust which will work its way into the folded metal and leave marks. With thicker metals a piercing saw can be used. The benefit of the piercing saw is that the edge is not distorted, so despite the dust it is a good option for precise shapes.

 7. Anneal the metal. Do not quench in water or pickle as water will get trapped into the fold and then transfer onto tools, causing them to rust. Instead, patiently wait for it to cool down until it can be handled. An easy way to speed up this cooling process is to place it on a piece of steel such as steel anvil. (If other people are working alongside you in the workshop, ensure you let them know the metal is hot.)

8. Open out the fold. It may be possible, if the metal is very thin, to prise it open with your fingers. An opening tool (such as a carved toothbrush handle,

see Chapter 1) can aid this. For particularly tricky pieces, support the folded metal in the vice, again protected with the vice jaws, open side up, and use a straight burnisher gently tapped with an old mallet to start the opening. Small, lightweight pieces will be able to be opened in one go, but larger more complex shapes or those made in thicker metal may require annealing again partway through opening. The decision to re-anneal can only be

Fig. 2.10 Confirming the fold by striking along the fold with the slightly domed side of the planishing hammer working on a steel flat plate.

Fig. 2.11 The resulting line fold.

made by feeling how much the metal is responding to being opened, so is something you learn with practice. There is no limit to the number of times the piece can be re-annealed so it is advisable to do so if you think it might be a good idea, rather than pushing the metal too far and causing it to crack.

9. At this point, you can decide how far to open the fold. If the metal is fully opened out, the fold can then be 'confirmed' by either planishing or passing through the rolling mill. This squares off the edge of the fold and can be useful if looking to create a geometric look; the raised fold can almost look like a square wire soldered onto a flat sheet of metal. However, you may choose to stop short of fully opening the fold, if you like the shape that reveals itself as you are opening out the metal. Once the folded form is fully opened out it can be pickled to remove oxides.

Fig. 2.12 'Leaf Bowls' in sterling silver by Louise Mary Muttitt, created using a line fold confirmed in the rolling mill.

Fig. 2.13 'Standing Salad Servers' in sterling silver by Louise Mary Muttitt, also created using a line fold confirmed in the rolling mill.

OPENING FOLDED FORMS

One of the more challenging aspects in fold forming is the opening out of the shapes once they have been forged. Thicker metals are harder to open, as are narrow pieces.

Invaluable tools for opening out folds are a vice protected with rubber jaws, a straight burnisher with a fine tip, and an opening tool made from a toothbrush handle. Additional tools include steel silversmithing stakes or a tapered ring mandrel, and jewellers' flat nylon pliers.

Be patient when opening out fold forming, as distorting the metal at this stage can easily spoil the form. The metal will workharden – especially along the fold – as it opens out, so re-annealing partway through can make it much easier. In practice the form does not always open out evenly at first. Once the form is pretty much opened out, the edges can be tweaked to refine the shape; this is easily done with thumbs and nylon pliers, which will not leave any marks on the metal.

Partial Fold

In this variation of the flat line fold, follow the steps above, but only fold and planish (or roll) the metal partway along, then anneal and open, to reveal a fold which stops in the middle of the sheet. This can be effective if repeated in different positions several times on the same piece of metal.

Fig. 2.14 **This fold has been compressed with the rolling mill halfway along to create a partial fold.**

Fig. 2.15 **The resulting partial fold.**

Fig. 2.16 **'Pair of Serving Spoons' by Louise Mary Muttitt in sterling silver, featuring the partial fold created using the rolling mill.**

Fig. 2.17 About 5mm of the fold is pinched in the vice, the metal is then opened out and malleted flat.

Fig. 2.18 This is the result once removed from the vice.

Fig. 2.19 Using a mallet to flatten one end of the protruding fold sideways.

Fig. 2.20 Using a mallet to flatten the other end of the fold sideways in the opposite direction.

Rolled-Over Line Fold

This is a variation on the flat line fold. It creates a fold that rolls from one side of the metal to the other, making the metal look like pleated fabric.

Tools & Materials

- 1 piece of copper sheet, 0.3–0.5mm thick
- Basic tool kit

1. Follow steps 1–7 for producing a flat line fold. It does not matter whether you choose to planish or roll to confirm the fold; however, using a rolling mill will give the cleanest look to the finished fold.

2. Insert the folded edge of the piece of copper into a vice, ensuring the vice jaws are protected with rubber or copper jaws, pinching about 5mm of the metal. Keeping it in the vice, open out the metal, initially with opening tools and then gently hammering it with a mallet so it is completely flat.

3. Take it out of the vice and place on the planishing block, the raised folded edge upwards. Now use a rubber or hide mallet to flatten one end of the protruding fold sideways, down onto the opened out metal, then flatten the other end in the other direction. This should result in a fold that rolls from one side to the other.

The closer the two ends are, the tighter the roll will be. Mallet towards the point where the fold crosses over to tighten the twist.

Fig. 2.21 The resulting rolled over line fold.

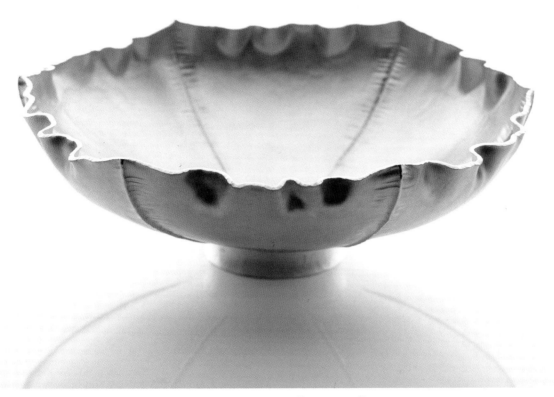

Fig. 2.22 'Six Fold Bowl' by Rauni Higson, Britannia silver, 22cm diameter.

Forged Folds

Forged folds take the simple line fold to the next level, and start to really push the properties of sheet metal. They can produce very interesting three-dimensional forms, which strongly visually reference forms found in nature. Experimenting with forged folds can be very exciting, as very dynamic changes occur to the metal, and relatively quickly too, especially if working on quite a small scale. Because of this, prototypes for new designs can be explored rapidly. Many designers leave the hammer marks in the finished pieces as evidence of the process. These forged folds are what metalsmiths most commonly refer to as fold forming, and there are many artists and designers creating stunning works around the world.

Forging the fold can be done on either the open or the folded edge. Forging the open edge produces open leaf-like forms, whereas forging along the folded edge produces more enclosed shell-like spirals. Long, narrow pieces curve more dramatically and quickly, so to make the process more exciting, follow the guideline dimensions given in the step-by-step guide for the first samples. Make two at once so that you can compare how different the form is that arises from forging on the open as opposed to the folded edge, and as you can be working on one while the other cools from annealing it takes very little extra time.

Fig. 2.23 Starting to forge the open edge of the folded copper strip, working outwards from the centre as indicated by the arrows drawn in marker pen.

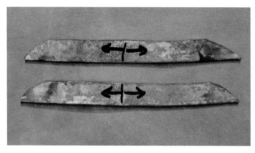

Fig. 2.24 Two identical copper pieces, folded and ready for forging, the open edge upwards on both pieces.

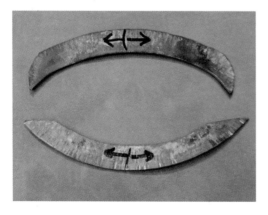

Fig. 2.25 The two same copper pieces after one round of forging, where the top one has been forged on the open edge and the bottom one has been forged along the folded edge.

Basic Forged Folds

Tools & Materials

- 2 pieces of copper sheet, approx. 100mm x 20mm, 0.3–0.5mm thick
- Basic tool kit

1. Follow steps 1–4 for the flat line fold, folding along the length, therefore ending up with two pieces, each measuring approximately 100mm x 10mm.

2. Cut a taper on either end of the two folded strips with snips.

3. Using a marker pen, draw a line along the middle of each of the sides. This acts as a guide while hammering.

4. The edge that you forge will stretch, so with your first strip, decide whether to hammer along either the folded edge or the open edge. Place this edge in line with the curved edge of the steel flat plate or edge of the anvil. Start forging, making strikes at 90° to this edge, working from the middle outwards towards the taper, then start from the middle and work out in the other direction towards the other end. The metal will stretch along the hammered edge, causing the metal to curve as it grows longer on this edge while the

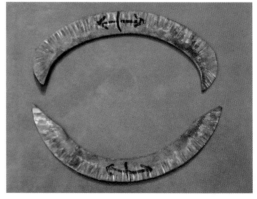

Fig. 2.26 The same two copper pieces after a second round of forging.

Fig. 2.27 The same two copper pieces after a third round of forging.

Fig. 2.28 The two pieces were opened up after three rounds of forging; as they are opened out they curve more.

unhammered edge stays the same. As the metal curves, you will need to ensure you always keep the hammer blows at 90° to the edge of the metal. To achieve this, it is easiest to move the metal being forged with the supporting hand while keeping the hammering consistent and even with the dominant hand. When hammering along the folded edge, keep the hammer blows just inside the fold itself, as striking too close to the fold will weaken the fold, which may result in it cracking when it is opened. Turn the piece over and repeat in exactly the same way on the other side, working along the same edge. Now repeat with the second strip of metal, this time choosing to forge the opposite edge to the first strip.

5. The metal will have work-hardened, so anneal at this point. Leave to cool down naturally; do not quench or pickle. Repeat the hammering (as in step 4) as many times as you wish, annealing between each round, until you are happy with the curve you have produced. Three rounds is a good amount to aim for with your first samples.

6. Anneal and allow to cool, then open the form out using your fingers, perhaps using a burnisher to 'encourage' the form to open and reveal itself.

You will find that the piece curves more as you open it out, particularly those pieces that have been forged along the fold. The more dramatic the curve and the thicker the metal, the harder opening out will be, and the piece may need re-annealing partway through the process. Consider wearing gloves to protect your fingers, because if the piece has become very thin on the folded edge this is prone to cracking and edges can also be very sharp if it has been forged very thin.

7. Once the form has been opened out it can be pickled and finished as required.

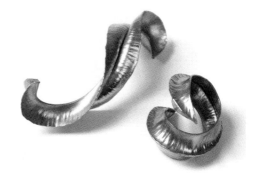

Fig. 2.29 The two pieces after being pickled and brass wire brushed.

Forged Folds – Ruffled Leaves

If you are interested in creating shapes that look like leaves, this technique is a good way to enhance the forged fold above. By forging in interspersed points along the open edge, it produces a ruffled edge, which gives a leaf-like quality to the metal forms. Accurate hammering is required to make this technique work most effectively.

Fig. 2.30 'Sweet Pea Bangle' by Rauni Higson, sterling silver. In this bangle forging has been used to create the rippled edges to resemble the delicacy of sweet pea petals.

Tools & Materials

- 1 piece of copper sheet, approx. 60mm x 40mm, 0.3–0.5mm thick
- Basic tool kit

1. Follow steps 1–4 for the flat line fold, folding along the length, therefore ending up with a piece which measures approximately 60mm x 20mm.

2. Use snips to cut the open edge into a curve, the profile of half a leaf; the exact shape of this curve is up to you.

3. Hammer along the open edge of the metal. As with the forged fold above, start in the middle and work evenly outwards towards the edge, then start from the middle and work out in the other direction towards the other edge. The metal will have begun to stretch along this hammered edge, forcing the metal to curve as it grows longer on this edge while the folded edge stays the same length. Turn the metal over and repeat in exactly the same way on the other side, working along the same edge.

4. Anneal the metal and allow it to cool. With a marker pen, draw a series of radiating lines

Fig. 2.31 The first round of forging has been carried out in this piece of copper, which will become a ruffled leaf.

Fig. 2.32 Drawing on the radiating lines with a fine marker pen.

Fig. 2.33 Forging directly on the lines.

Fig. 2.34 The ruffled leaf once opened up.

about 10mm apart, matching them on both sides of the metal. For the next round of forging, only hammer on these lines. Turn the piece over and repeat on the other side, a little harder on this second round. The areas which are being hammered become hardened, and the pieces between remain annealed, so the softer metal ripples upwards.

5. Open the leaf out, perhaps using a burnisher to encourage initially, then your fingers. A leaf with naturally ruffled edges should be revealed. Tweak the shaping of the ruffled edges if required with round-nosed nylon pliers.

Quick Forging
– Using a Rolling Mill

The rolling mill can be used to create forged folds with the addition of a strip of card, and has the added benefits of being both quick and adding an interesting texture to the surface of the metal at the same time. As well as using card, it would be possible to experiment with other materials to try to produce the same effect but with more varied textures, for example fabric or ribbons. It would also be possible to use another piece of metal to forge the fold. As with the forged folds, using long narrow pieces will create more prominent curves.

Tools & Materials

• 1 piece of copper sheet, approx. 60mm x 40mm, 0.3–0.5mm thick
• Basic tool kit
• Strip of lightweight card, approx. 80mm x 15mm

1. Follow steps 1–4 for the flat line fold, folding along the length, therefore ending up with a piece of metal which measures approximately 60mm x 20mm.

2. Fold the piece of card in half along its length. Tuck either the folded or open edge of the metal

Fig. 2.35 Two folded strips of lightweight card and two folded pieces of copper ready for quick forging using the rolling mill.

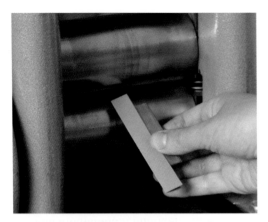

Fig. 2.36 Passing one copper piece half wrapped in a piece of folded card.

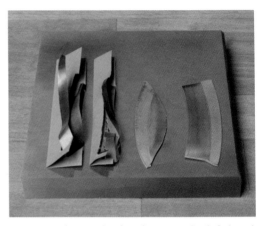

Fig. 2.37 The result after forging. The left-hand copper sample had the card wrapped over the folded edge, and the right-hand copper sample had the card wrapped around the open edge. The pressure needs to be quite tight for this to work effectively, as shown by the way the card has become thin and torn where it has come into contact with the edge of the copper.

inside the folded card and pass through the rolling mill. As a guide, set the rolling mill to double the original metal thickness, so for metal that is 0.5mm thick, set the rolling mill to 1mm. The edge which has the card wrapped around it will be thinned more than the exposed metal, causing it to stretch along this edge. The card will also produce a contrasting texture on the surface of the metal.

3. Anneal, allow to cool, then open out the metal to reveal the shape. The metal should curve more as it is opened.

Fig. 2.38 The difference between the two samples can be seen more clearly once they have been opened up. Again, as brass wire brush has been used to bring up a lustre on the surface, this highlights how textured the surface of the metal has become where the card came into contact with it. The remaining copper, which came into contact with the rolling mill, remains smooth and bright.

Curved Folds

The folds we have looked at so far have started as straight lines. Another interesting area to explore is creating curved folds.

Wire Groove Curved Fold

This wonderfully simple technique presents many creative possibilities and can be used to create matching pieces, making it ideal for small-scale batch production such as a series of identical necklace links. Thinnest sheet works most effectively for this technique; the example in Figs. 2.39 to 2.43 was made using 0.25mm-thick sheet copper.

Tools & Materials
- 1 piece of copper sheet, 0.2–0.4mm thick
- Binding wire
- Masking tape
- Basic tool kit

1. Cut a piece of binding wire about 80mm longer than your piece of metal. Using your hands or round-nosed pliers, curve a length of binding wire into the shape of the folded edge you would like to create. Tape either end of the wire down onto an old steel flat plate with masking tape.

2. Anneal, pickle, rinse and dry the piece of copper sheet. Place this on top of the binding wire.

3. Using the flat polished face of a planishing hammer, start in the centre and hammer along the sheet of copper, following the line of the binding wire underneath. Then go back to the centre and work outwards in the other direction. When you lift the piece of copper, you will see that the line of binding wire has been deeply imprinted onto the underside of the copper.

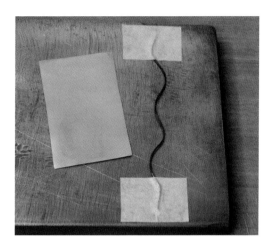

Fig. 2.39 Taping the shaped binding wire to an old flat plate.

Fig. 2.40 Planishing along the flat sheet of copper following the line of the wire underneath, a shiny line emerges.

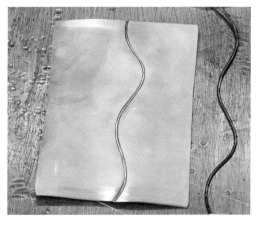

Fig. 2.41 On the reverse side a groove has been formed in the sheet metal.

4. Anneal, pickle, rinse and dry the piece of copper sheet. With the indentation facing downwards, use your hands to bend the metal downwards either side of the line, revealing a curved fold that matches the shape of the binding wire. The tighter the curve, the harder the metal will be to bend. Re-anneal as necessary while shaping.

Fig. 2.42 With the groove facing downwards, bend down either side of the line using hands.

Fig. 2.43 The resulting curved fold after two rounds of annealing and bending using hands.

Scored Curved Folds

Scored folds is the traditional metalsmithing technique used to make boxes. Scoring a curved line in sheet metal takes some skill and practice. An easier technique is to use a cutting disc in a pendant motor to cut a groove into the metal sheet. This technique has the advantage of not distorting the other side of your piece of metal, therefore if you would like to incorporate subtle textures into your design, for example by etching or rolling a pattern onto the metal, then this can be done first. As with the wire groove fold, softer curves will be easier to fold after scoring.

Once cut, the metal is weakened and therefore far more prone to cracking, so make sure you anneal the metal before folding up. While annealing, make sure to flux the scored lines to prevent oxides building up in the recesses, as the pickle will not be able to reach into the groove once it is folded. Because metal is removed from inside the fold by scoring, this is one of the only folds that requires soldering to strengthen.

Tools & Materials

- 1 piece of copper sheet, 0.7mm thick
- Pendant motor fitted with a cutting disc
- Basic tool kit

1. On the reverse side of your metal, mark out the position of the curved fold by drawing a line with a scribe. Run the scribe through the line a few times to define it clearly.

2. Wearing goggles, use the pendant motor fitted with the separating disc to score the groove in the metal, following the line you have marked out.

3. Paint along the groove with flux, then anneal.

4. Pickle the metal while still flat, rinse and dry.

Fig. 2.44 Using a pendant motor to create a curved groove fold.

Fig. 2.45 The resulting fold after folding and soldering.

5. With the groove facing downwards, use your hands to bend the metal downwards either side of the line, revealing a curved fold.

6. Once the metal is folded to the degree you are happy with, flux the grooves again and flood with solder to strengthen the fold.

Single Line Folds Development

The folds outlined in this chapter form the basis of fold forming. Having tried some of them out, now consider how you might develop your own designs using these techniques. Perhaps a fold could be repeated a number of times in a piece, or try combining two or more techniques in a single piece. Altering proportions can also be interesting, such as making very long, thin folds.

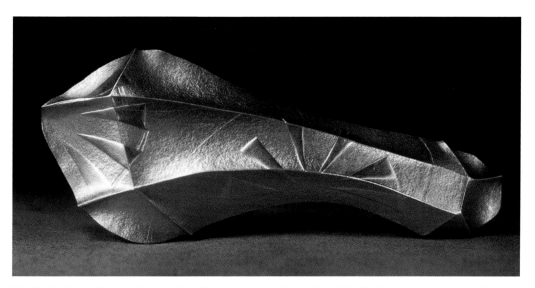

Fig. 2.46 'Scored Brooch' in gold by Charles Lewton-Brain, in which the texture was applied by roll printing before scoring and folding.

MULTIPLE FOLDS

Having understood the basic concept of fold forming by exploring different methods and types of single folds in Chapter 2, this chapter moves onto the techniques used to explore the creation of multiple folds in sheet metal. These are divided into two sections: multiple folds where hammers are used to confirm and forge the folds, and multiple folds that use the rolling mill to forge the folds.

By suggesting relatively small pieces of metal for the step-by-step instructions, it helps to keep the processes quick, allowing understanding of each particular technique to be gained in a short amount of time. Many of these multiple folds become more dynamic and exciting when the scale is increased, allowing more folds to be added or the folds to be made longer, so do play around with the dimensions and number of folds as you try developing these folds for your own designs.

Multiple Folds Using Hammers

Basic T-Fold

An ideal starting point in this category is the T-fold, where two folds are created at once. I was taught both the basic T-fold and the wedge T-fold by renowned metalsmith Cynthia Eid, while she was in the UK teaching a summer course at Birmingham School of Jewellery a few years ago. The T-fold is the basis for some very interesting explorations, which include chasing on air (*see* box, 'Chasing on Air'). The name was given to this type of fold because of how it appears from the side when it is held in the vice. The folded edges that we are working with are at either end of the top of the 'T'. The stem of the 'T' is the part that drops down into the vice.

Before beginning, cover the vice jaws with folded copper or brass sheet, as leaving the vice jaws exposed will mark the metal being fold formed, and rubber vice jaws are too soft for forging onto. For a first attempt, try making two identical pieces up to stage 6, then open one without annealing first and one after annealing to see the different results.

Tools & Materials
- 1 piece of copper sheet, 80mm x 60mm, 0.3–0.5mm thick
- Basic tool kit

1. Anneal, pickle, rinse and dry the sheet metal.

2. Bend the piece of sheet loosely so that the two long edges come together.

3. Place the two long edges in a vice, leaving a soft loop shape extending above the vice. Make sure there is a fair amount of metal held in the vice, as this will give leverage when opening the fold out after forming.

Fig. 3.1 **The first step in creating a T-fold is to put the copper in a loose loop in the vice. The vice jaws have sheet copper pieces as jaw protectors.**

Fig. 3.2 **Malleting the two ends of the loop.**

Fig. 3.3 **Malleting the table flat.**

Fig. 3.4 **Planishing along the two edges to confirm the fold.**

4. Beginning at one end, use a mallet to push one end of the loop down flat on the top of the vice. Then repeat at the other end. The middle should be rounded and look like a pillow.

5. Now mallet along the rest of the metal (squashing the pillow) with the mallet until it is completely flat. You have now created the basic T-fold, with the ends of the metal held in the vice referred to as the 'legs'. The top of the T – the surface area you can see when the metal is still in the vice – is known as the 'table' and there are two folds running along each side. Use a planishing hammer to confirm these two folds by hammering along each of them once.

6. Remove the formed metal from the vice, and then choose whether to open straight away, or anneal first then open the folds, as each will produce a different result. If the T-fold is opened without annealing the metal first, the table remains flat as it is hard and rigid from being worked. However, if it is annealed before opening, the table will bend downwards and the legs move upwards, creating a very different form.

Fig. 3.5 **Two identical T-folds. The left-hand sample was opened out without annealing and the right-hand sample was opened out after annealing.**

Fig. 3.6 Forging along the folded edges of the T-fold while it is held by hand and supported on a flat plate.

Fig. 3.7 The resulting T-fold after forging.

T-Fold Variations

Forging the T-Fold

Instead of simply planishing to confirm the two folded edges, use a forging hammer to forge the two folded edges while the piece is still in the vice, causing them to stretch. Then anneal and open out to reveal the form.

Fig. 3.8 Creating an asymmetrical T-fold by knocking the loop off-centre before malleting the ends flat.

Forging the folds of the T-fold can also be done without the vice. Follow the steps above up to 5, then take the T-fold out of the vice and start forging the folds freely, for example supported on the edge of a planishing block. This will give quite a different result as both sides of the metal are free to move, so both the legs and the table become distorted, creating a more twisted and organic effect.

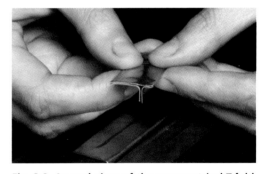

Fig. 3.9 An end view of the asymmetrical T-fold after confirming.

Asymmetrical T-Fold

The 'T' doesn't have to be symmetrical. Before beginning stage 4, use the mallet to push the protruding loop off centre, then continue to create the T-fold as above, and work into the folds by planishing or forging as required.

Wedge T-Fold

This is also created in a very similar way to the basic T-fold, except that the loop of metal (stage 3) is placed in the vice at an angle, so that when it is hammered flat the table is triangular instead of rectangular. The wedge T-fold can then be treated like the original T-fold, so it can be confirmed by planishing, or forged either while still in the vice, or, for a more organic form, remove from the vice and forge against the edge of an anvil.

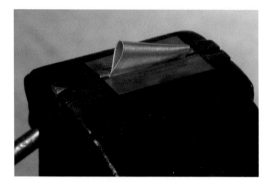

Fig. 3.10 To create a wedge T-fold the loop needs to be held in the vice at an angle.

Fig. 3.11 The wedge T-fold after malleting flat.

Fig. 3.12 The resulting wedge T-fold once annealed and opened.

CHASING ON AIR

If you follow the steps for creating a T-fold up to step 4 you will create what is known as a 'pillow'. This shape is an ideal starting point for repoussé or chasing on air. As no pitch is used, this is much cleaner and quicker than traditional chasing. Work into it as you would a normal chasing, by using larger punches first then working in the finer detail. As the metal hardens during chasing, remove from the vice and anneal, then continue. The amount of times you need to anneal will be dependent on the complexity of the chased pattern. Working at an angle around the edges first will help to keep the pillow taller and so will increase the variance in depth that can be created.

If you do not have any chasing punches, you can still create some really interesting patterns and deep relief effects using steel doming punches, unusual hammers with textured or rounded faces and letter punches.

Once your chased pattern is complete, the chased section can be cut out, but perhaps consider how you could incorporate the T-folds into the finished piece.

Chasing on air can also be done equally as effectively on a wedge T-fold.

Fig. 3.13 Chasing onto the pillow formed in the early stages of creating a T-fold.

Fig. 3.14 Working in finer detail with a line punch.

Romero Fold

For a beautiful organic leaf form with a raised centre spine, try making this variation of the wedge T-fold, in which the 'legs' – the part held in the vice – are forged. This fold is one of many folds that have been named after the person who developed them. Do not use anything harder than brass wire for step 5 if you are using a planishing hammer, as striking a harder metal could damage the face of the hammer.

Fig. 3.15 To begin the Romero fold, create a small loop at an angle as with a wedge T-fold.

Fig. 3.16 The narrow wedge once it has been malleted and confirmed.

Tools & Materials

- 1 piece of copper sheet, 40mm x 60mm, approx. 0.3mm thick
- Straightened brass wire, 1mm thick, at least 80mm long
- Masking tape
- Basic tool kit

1. Anneal, pickle, rinse and dry the sheet metal.

2. Bend the piece of sheet loosely so that the two long edges come together.

3. Place the two long edges in a vice at a slight angle, leaving a small loop shape extending above the vice.

4. Mallet flat, which will create a long, narrow tapered table. Planish along the two folded edges to confirm the two folds.

5. Now rest the piece of brass wire on top of the table, and tape it into position at either end. Use a planishing hammer and work along the wire to create a groove in line with the opening of the vice.

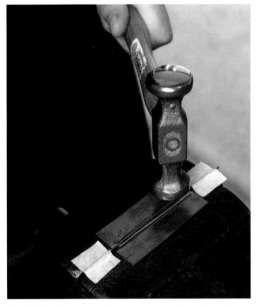

Fig. 3.17 A piece of brass wire is taped in line with the vice jaw opening, then planish along the wire forcing the copper sheet down into the gap between the two jaws.

6. Remove the wire and the metal from the vice. Use snips to cut a curved edge on the open side.

7. Working on a steel planishing block, use a raising hammer to forge the open edge from the centre outwards. Repeat both sides.

8. Anneal, allow to cool, then open, using fingers to begin with. Starting at the wider end, use a pair of flat-nosed pliers to pull the two folded edges of the table towards each other and to expose the centre spine that was created by planishing the wire along the centre of the table. The leaf-like form should be revealed.

Variation

Add ruffles using the 'Ruffled Leaves' technique in Chapter 2 as an added detail to the Romero Fold.

Fig. 3.18 **Forging the open edge of the leaf.**

Fig. 3.19 **The resulting leaf after opening with raised centre spine.**

Cross Fold

The cross fold is the next step on from a T-fold and its variations, as this creates three parallel folds at once in a sheet of metal. Like the T-fold, they can be made at an angle as well as straight.

Tools & Materials
- 1 piece of copper sheet, 80mm x 60mm, 0.3–0.5mm thick
- Basic tool kit
- A piece of steel rod (or tool handle equivalent)

1. Anneal, pickle, rinse and dry the sheet metal.

2. Bend the piece of sheet loosely so that the two long edges come together.

3. Place the two long edges in a vice, leaving a soft loop shape extending above the vice. The larger the loop, the further apart the three resulting folds will be. It is possible to make the loop quite small.

4. Making sure the loop stays centred, use the flat side of a planishing hammer to strike along the loop on both sides at 45°, to form a soft peak; when looking side on, the shape is triangular. Remove from the vice and anneal.

5. Once the metal has cooled, reposition it in the vice as before. Take a piece of round steel bar (if you do not have a piece of steel, a tool handle would work, for example the handle of a steel doming punch) and hold it in line with the vice jaws halfway up one of the sides and mallet it so that the flattened side creases inwards. Use either a mallet or a non-precious hammer such as an engineer's hammer with a flat face. Do not use a planishing hammer as the steel will mark the polished hammer face. Keep changing sides, working gradually until the profile from the end looks like a cross.

Fig. 3.20 Beginning the cross fold by using a planishing hammer to form a triangular prism shape above the vice.

Fig. 3.21 Using a steel bar struck with a mallet to collapse the prism walls inwards.

Fig. 3.22 Confirming the fold.

Fig. 3.23 The cross fold viewed from the end before opening.

6. Remove from the vice. There are now three folds, which can be simply confirmed with a planishing hammer; alternatively some or all of them can be forged. Once confirming or forging is complete, anneal and open to reveal three parallel folds.

Tapered Cross Fold

A tapered cross fold works effectively when used to create shaping around the edge of a bowl.

Fig. 3.24 **After folding the annealed copper square in half diagonally, planish to confirm the fold.**

Fig. 3.25 **After opening, fold in half again bringing the two opposite corners to meet, and work at the edge of the flat plate to confirm the fold with a planishing hammer.**

Four-Pointed Star Fold

A star fold is a good example of repeating two single flat line folds in a single sheet of metal. It can then be further developed using forging.

Tools & Materials

- 1 piece of copper sheet, 50mm x 50mm, 0.4mm thick
- Basic tool kit

1. Anneal, pickle, rinse and dry the metal. Fold in half diagonally, so that two corners meet. Working on a steel flat plate or anvil, mallet the fold closed, then planish to confirm the fold. Anneal and allow to cool.

2. Open out the fold, using an opening tool to get started, then opening out as far as possible using your fingers. Now working along a 90° edge (for example, on the steel flat plate), push down to make a fold running between the opposite two corners.

3. Use a mallet to compress this fold, missing out the very centre of the fold where the first fold crosses the new fold, then confirm the

Fig. 3.26 **With the folded edges facing downwards, use the 90° edge of the flat plate and your hands to push the metal up towards the centre of the star. Turn and repeat this on all four sides, and the four-pointed star form will begin to emerge.**

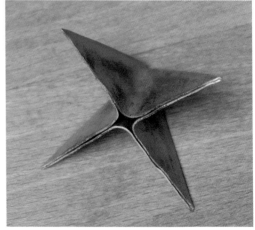

Fig. 3.27 **The closed star after folding is complete.**

Fig. 3.28 The closed star after two rounds of forging along all four of the folded edges, prior to opening.

Fig. 3.29 The resulting star form after opening gently with the tip of a straight burnisher.

fold using a planishing hammer. Anneal for a third time and allow to cool before opening out again using an opening tool to get started, then your fingers.

4. Turn the piece of metal so the folded edges are facing down and again use the 90° edge and your hands to push the metal up in the opposite direction, creating a bend which starts at the cross-over of the two folds and ends up at the centre of the straight edge. Turn and repeat this on all four sides, and the four-pointed star form will begin to emerge.

5. Use the anvil or flat plate again to flatten the sides of the star to further define the shape. This gives a basic four-pointed star shape, which is ready for forging. There are so many variations possible depending upon whether forging is done on the folds or along the open edges, as there are four of each to choose from. Once forged, open the shape a little to reveal the form created.

Multiple Folds Using the Rolling Mill

Here are two folded forms that can be created quite rapidly using the rolling mill. Both work best if the initial folding is accurate.

Heistad Cup

The Heistad cup is a really good use of the rolling mill for creating a three-dimensional form using multiple folds, as the rolling mill forges all the folds evenly at once.

Tools & Materials
- 1 square piece of copper sheet, 60mm x 60mm, 0.3–0.5mm thick
- Basic tool kit
- Rolling mill

1. Anneal, pickle, rinse and dry the metal sheet.

Fig. 3.30 Folding the square in half so the corners meet.

Fig. 3.31 After folding a second time.

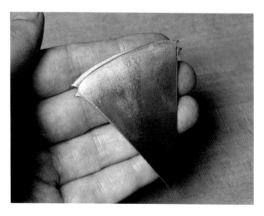

Fig. 3.32 After passing it through the rolling mill until it is around twice as long as the original folded metal.

2. Fold the metal corner to corner.

3. Flatten with a mallet on a steel planishing block or anvil, creating an isosceles triangle with two open sides, with one 90° corner and two 45° corners.

4. Fold the triangle in half again, bringing the two 45° corners together.

5. Flatten with a mallet, especially along the folded edges. This should make a smaller isosceles triangle, the same shape as before.

6. Set the rolling mill to four times the thickness of your original metal, and pass the folded triangle through, sending the 90° corner first.

7. Anneal the metal and allow it to cool down. Reduce the width of the rolling mill, and pass the metal through a second time, with the same point going in first.

8. Repeat step 7 at least once, but more times if you wish. The more times it is passed through the rolling mill, the more dynamic the resulting cup will be. Aim to at least double the length of the metal.

Fig. 3.33 The Heistad cup after annealing and opening.

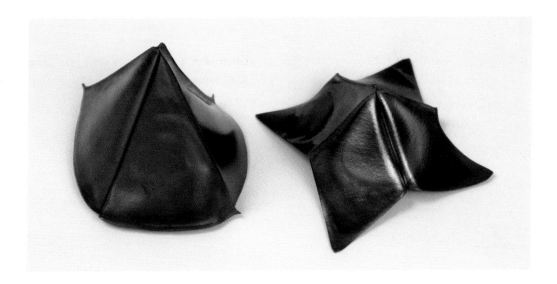

Fig. 3.34 Two Heistad cups: the left started with a square folded corner to corner, the right one was folded edge to edge twice so that before rolling the piece was a square exactly a quarter of the size of the original square.

9. Anneal and then gently open the cup. Pliers might be needed to begin with, but try to use your fingers as much as possible to prevent the metal from being marked.

Heistad Cup Variation

Start with a square of metal as before, but fold from edge to edge twice instead of corner to corner, so that rolling begins with a square that is a quarter of the size of the original sheet. Point the corner that is the centre of the sheet into the rolling mill first and forge in the same way as the original Heistad cup. The resulting form will have a cup with four diamond-shaped sides instead of triangles.

Fig. 3.35 Annealing copper while the metal is still folded up can often produce some wonderful iridescent surface colourings.

Fig. 3.36 These 'Bud Beakers' by Emma Jane Rule are made from Britannia silver and measure around 10cm in height. After following the process for making a Heistad Cup, they were annealed once more, wrapped in fabric and rolled to imprint the fabric texture onto the surface. After unfolding, a base is set to create a functional, decorative beaker.

Fig. 3.37 Copper versions of the 'Bud Beakers' by Emma Jane Rule, which measure around 10cm in height. These were made in the same way as her Britannia silver versions, and the surface texture has been further enhanced by patinating the copper using liver of sulphur and gently rubbed back.

Fig. 3.38 The Plunkett fold starts in the same way as a wedge T-fold, with a tapered table which has been malleted flat.

Fig. 3.39 Malleting the protruding side of the table to 45°.

Plunkett Fold

Kevin Plunkett developed this fold in the mid-1980s, which makes it one of the earliest named folds. The first few steps are identical to creating the wedge T-fold.

Tools & Materials

- 1 square piece of copper sheet, 80mm x 60mm, 0.3–0.5mm thick
- Basic tool kit
- Rolling mill

1. Anneal, pickle, rinse and dry the sheet metal.

2. Bend the piece of sheet loosely so that the two long edges come together.

3. Place the two long edges in a vice at an angle, leaving a soft loop shape extending above the vice at one end and the top of the loop level with the top of the vice at the other end.

4. Mallet down to create the triangular-shaped table as with a wedge T-fold.

Fig. 3.40 Repeating with the other side of the table.

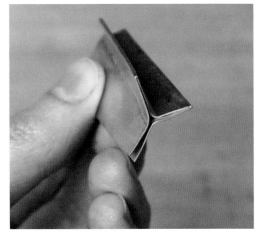

Fig. 3.41 The Plunkett fold viewed from the end before completely closing up.

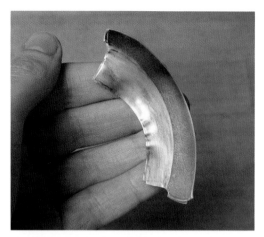

Fig. 3.42 The Plunkett fold after it has been passed through the rolling mill.

Fig. 3.43 The Plunkett fold once opened out; notice how it has curved more as it has opened.

5. Now remove the metal from the vice and reposition so that one side of the table is held in the vice. Mallet the protruding side of the table down towards the top of the vice but away from the 'legs', to about a 45° angle.

6. Remove from the vice and repeat with the other side of the table. The side profile should now be a 'Y' shape instead of a 'T'.

7. Remove from the vice again and now, working on a flat plate, close the two arms of the 'Y' and flatten the piece of metal completely.

8. Pass it through the rolling mill several times, reducing the thickness each time so that the metal stretches and begins to curve. It is more effective if you put the pointed end in first.

9. Anneal and open gently with your hands to reveal the curved Plunkett fold.

LEFT: **Fig. 3.44 'Fold-Formed Pendant' by Charles Lewton-Brain, aluminium.**

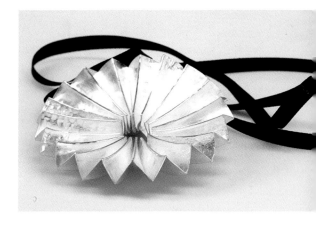

RIGHT: **Fig. 3.45 'Emmadalion Pendant' made from sterling silver by Emma Jane Rule, measuring 7cm in diameter. This piece was also created from multiple pleated sections of silver, each folded in a concertina, forged, opened and then soldered together.**

Pleated Folds

Take multiple folds a step further and create pleated folds for an ambitious approach to fold forming. Use thinner gauges of metal particularly for initial experiments and fold the metal into a concertina. Once folded, forge the folds simultaneously. Because multiple layers are forged at the same time, the changes in the resulting form once it is opened out are very dynamic.

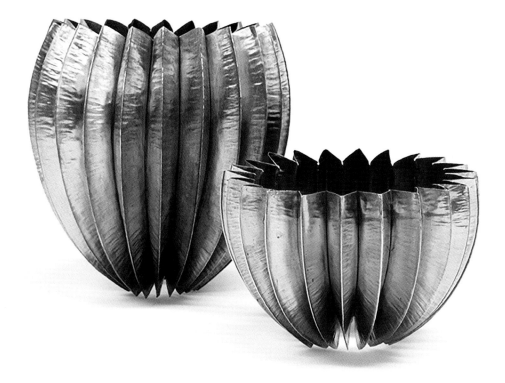

Fig. 3.46 'Prickled Pods' by Emma Jane Rule, made from copper, measuring 16cm and 9cm tall. These pods are made from multiple sections of pleated copper that has been forged along one edge to curve the metal. After opening, the folded sections are then soldered together and manipulated by hand into their final form.

MICRO FOLDING

Background

Micro folding is also referred to as metal corrugation. Although there is a little cross-over with the fold forming from Chapters 2 and 3, metal corrugation really falls into a separate category of its own. Patricia McAleer is the leading metalsmith who has done extensive research and development in this field internationally. I was introduced to micro folding by Cynthia Eid, who has also done considerable work with this technique. The scale of micro folding, as the name suggests, is quite small and so most suited to jewellery and small work.

Inspiration for metalwork designs incorporating micro folding can come from a variety of sources. In the natural world, many structures and forms are found which represent ripples or corrugation, for example ripples in the sand or the ridges of a scallop shell. There is a wide range of manmade sources of inspiration too: we can look at textiles and paper crafts, as well as engineering and product designs where corrugation has been used to solve practical problems, corrugated card and corrugated iron being two of the most successful uses of this engineering technique.

Corrugation is used so extensively essentially because it makes a thin material much stronger and very difficult to bend perpendicular to the ridges. As less material is required, structures are cheaper to produce and have the added benefit of being lighter too. This same advantage applies to jewellery making, and so thin gauges of metals can be used to create pieces which are

Fig. 4.1 Corrugation on a roof shows a practical use of corrugation.

Fig. 4.2 Corrugated iron cladding on a barn.

strong yet not heavy. A thinner gauge of metal sheet can therefore be employed, making it an economical way of working in more expensive precious materials such as silver and gold. Corrugation also seems to make pieces feel more substantial due to their structural strength.

Fig. 4.3 Shells can be inspiring forms for corrugation.

Fig. 4.4 Hosta leaves are another example of an inspiring natural form for metal corrugation.

For those with an engineering mind, micro folding can be approached in a methodical and mathematical manner, whereby you can calculate accurately how much your pieces will shrink from the original sheet size. It can also be approached in a freer, more experimental way, and, with the addition of other metalsmithing techniques, corrugation can provide the basis for very rigid geometric designs through to irregular and more organic looking forms. It is therefore a technique that appeals to a vast range of design styles.

Corrugators

Micro folding requires specialist equipment, in particular a set of rollers for corrugation. The most ideal tool for the jeweller's workshop is the Bonny Doon Micro-Fold Brake. For the examples and instruction on micro folding in this chapter, this Micro-Fold Brake has been used unless otherwise specified. Below are detailed explanations on this and other tools that can be used to create metal corrugation on a jeweller's scale, including tube wringers and paper crimping machines.

Micro-Fold Brake

The Bonny Doon Engineering Micro-Fold Brake has been designed specifically for jewellery-scale corrugation. At the time of writing, there is not a UK supplier for this tool, but they can be ordered from tool shops in the USA offering international delivery (*see* Appendix for details on suppliers).

The Micro-Fold Brake consists of two interlocking rollers, which are made of hardened and anodized steel to prevent roller damage and rusting. The lower roller is fixed, while the upper roller can be adjusted to accommodate different thicknesses of metals in much the same way as a rolling mill. The brake can be fixed to the bench with screws or, if you do not have a permanent space available in your workshop, it can either be clamped to the edge of a bench with G-clamps or held securely in a vice.

This tool is a good size, as the rollers are 8" (203mm) wide, so it can be used to corrugate metal up to this width. It is suitable for using with softer metals, such as silver alloys, gold alloys and copper. Harder metals such as yellow brass, nickel silver and titanium are not suitable as they will mark the rollers. Ideal thicknesses of metal sheet are 0.2mm to 0.5mm. Thicker sheet metal can be used but only in narrow strips. It is important to note that the metal must always be annealed before corrugation; this applies to all the corrugators.

It is also possible to corrugate wires using the Micro-Fold Brake. The manufacturers recommend doing this at the sides just in case it damages the rollers in any way, leaving the centre for rolling sheet metal.

Other Metal Corrugators

At the time of writing, there are three other metal corrugators on the market suitable for small-scale work that may also be worth exploring, depending on your geographical location and budget. They all have the advantage of a proper rotation handle and the ability to be either bolted to a bench or held in a vice while corrugating.

The Profiform Proco, which is available in three different sizes, is manufactured by a Swiss firm with suppliers throughout Europe.

There is a small Italian-made metal corrugator also available called Zig Zag. The advantage with this particular rolling mill is that it has four different-sized corrugators that are finer than the Micro-Fold Brake, so it can be used for very delicate, intricate work. The disadvantage is that it is very narrow, so is more restrictive in the width of strips that can be used.

At the top end of the price range, British firm Durston manufacture a corrugation mill. This has the advantage of being a very substantial piece of equipment which can take thicker materials than any others.

Tube Wringer

One step down from the specialist metal corrugators is a tube wringer. This piece of equipment has been designed to extract products such as paint from paint tubes. These devices are normally hand-held. Make sure you source one

Fig. 4.5 The Bonny Doon Micro-Fold Brake.

Fig. 4.6 Italian-made Zig Zag machine for creating very small corrugation, approximately 2.7cm wide.

Fig. 4.7 Industrial tube wringer manufactured by Gill Mechanical Company.

Fig. 4.8 Paper crimper by Fiskars, with aluminium rollers.

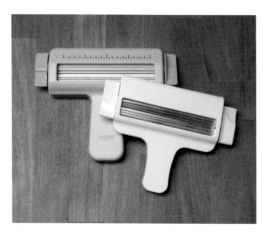

Fig. 4.9 Two paper crimpers, both with aluminium rollers.

Fig. 4.10 Wavy paper crimper. The rollers are plastic so it is really only suitable for very thin metal sheets.

with metal rollers as they will be more durable. One of the superior models is the TubeWringer 401 Heavy Duty, manufactured by Gill Mechanical Company and widely available, mainly from suppliers in the USA with worldwide delivery.

Paper Crimpers

If you are completely new to micro folding and unsure about making a larger investment in the metal corrugators described above, there are some small hand-held paper crimpers available that, although designed for paper and card, are substantial enough to corrugate thin copper sheet. If you are trying to source one, they are often called crimping machines and established craft tool manufacturers such as Do It Crafts and Fiskars have models. These tools, often made from plastic, are only suitable for very thin gauges of sheet metal; if you can find one with aluminium rollers, these are more durable. Like the tube wringers, paper crimpers are usually designed to be hand-held, however you may find that you can support them in a vice with care; it may be difficult to do so without damaging the outer casing, so use a pair of rubber vice jaws to protect the crimper. The other drawback with many paper crimpers is that you cannot usually adjust the distance between the two rollers.

Wavy paper crimping machines are a little more difficult to source and are currently only available in plastic, so they are really only suitable for the thinnest sheet metal up to 0.3mm.

Complementary Tools for Metal Corrugation

Confirming Pliers

A very useful tool for corrugation is a pair of specialist Swanstrom confirming pliers. These are available in three different widths: 1", 2" and 3". I recommend the 1" initially as they are suitable for a range of projects; add the other sizes as required.

These pliers have a wide jaw that tapers to a point, allowing you to insert them between the crests to pinch and confirm the corrugation. They have a parallel crimping action, meaning the crimp is straight and even. They also have soft-touch handles, which makes them very comfortable to use.

Fig. 4.11 1" Swanstrom Confirming Pliers, an invaluable tool for crimping metal corrugation.

Customized Flat Pliers

A pair of standard sprung flat pliers could be easily customized to create a narrower version of the specialist crimping pliers for a fraction of the cost. These would not be as effective in crimping wide sections as evenly, but could be used to good effect on smaller pieces. To customize your pliers, file the outside edge of the pliers to a fine taper as this will allow them to be inserted deep in the corrugated grooves, and soften the very top of the pliers slightly to prevent them from marking inside the grooves.

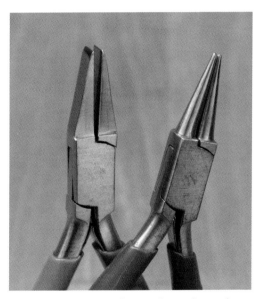

Fig. 4.12 Customized flat- and round-nosed pliers. The flat pair have been filed to a taper so that they can fit between corrugation, and the tips of the round-nosed pliers have been rounded so they do not mark the corrugation when smocking.

Customized Round-Nosed Pliers

For smocking, I have customized an inexpensive pair of sprung round-nosed pliers by rounding the tips with a file. These rounder tips do not make unsightly marks in the grooves of the corrugation when crimping to create patterns that look like smocking. Since customizing these pliers, I have discovered that they have lots of other uses in the workshop, and they only took a few minutes to create. I have since made a second pair from a finer tipped pair of round-nosed pliers for finer work.

Miscellaneous Tools

A further useful item is a soft brush, such as an old toothbrush, to brush over the rollers just before using in order to remove any dust or debris from previous use, as even the smallest specks create small indents on the surface of the metal when corrugating.

Small pieces of paper and card are also useful in corrugation to add texture, and for creating models to calculate blank sizes.

Opening tools used in fold forming will once again be useful when combining corrugation with fold forming.

From your basic tool kit, the following items can be used to add interest to corrugation:

- set of steel doming punches
- chasing and repoussé punches, pitch, pitch bowl and a chasing hammer
- ring mandrel (for making beads and corrugated wire chain links)
- drill to create holes prior to corrugation

Metals

Corrugation works best on thin sheet metal. I recommend using 0.3–0.5mm-thick sheet initially, and (as with fold forming) experimenting in copper first to try out ideas to get a feel for the technique and its possibilities.

Corrugation is really only suitable for soft metals – in particular I recommend silver alloys, gold alloys and copper. Hard metals, which include yellow brass, nickel silver and titanium, should be avoided as they will potentially damage the grooves of the corrugation tools.

It is also possible to corrugate sheet wax and use the wax models to cast in metal. This may be a particularly good use of plastic paper crimpers.

Terminology

The names given to the different parts of the corrugation will help with understanding the instructions in this chapter, particularly the more complex crimping patterns.

When looking side-on at the corrugation, the *crest* is the highest point and the *trough* is the lowest point. The size of the corrugation can be described in terms of *pitch*, which is the distance between each crest, and the depth, which is the distance from the top of a crest to the bottom of a trough when seen in profile.

Corrugation when it has been used as a solution in engineering has also been referred to as fluting or crimping. In this book, *crimping* is the term used to describe the closing or confirming of the ridges using pliers. This technique is also known as *confirming* as it tightens the fold in much the same way as the term was used to describe compressing folds in Chapter 2.

Calculating the Blank Size

When sheet metal or wire passes through the corrugator, the two halves of the tool push the metal down into the troughs and up over the crests, which means that the length of the original metal shrinks lengthways once corrugated, but retains the same width. In practice the length of the metal piece that you start with will reduce in length by somewhere between a quarter and a third. This means that if you want to create a precise shape, such as a circle, you would need to start with an oval that is 25 per cent to 33 per cent longer than the final shape. The exact amount will depend on the tool you are using, the thickness of the metal and how tight the rollers are. If the piece you are creating is going to be crimped (this is when all the crests are squeezed together), the metal length will decrease even further – after crimping it will be a little over a third of the original length, but again this is only an estimate and will vary according to the same factors.

A quick method to get an idea of the size metal you need is to make a paper template and corrugate that; it can then be flattened out and used as a template to cut the metal blank from. This will be pretty close but not absolutely precise. If you are aiming for a very precise shape, or planning to make a piece in an expensive precious metal such as gold, you would save wastage by making up a test piece in copper in the exact same thickness so that the blank can be cut accurately from gold prior to corrugation.

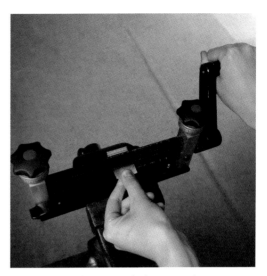

Fig. 4.13 Passing annealed copper sheet through the Bonny Doon Micro-Fold Brake.

Basic Corrugation

In the set of instructions below I have included advice on preparing the rollers and the metal that are not repeated in as much depth in other processes to save repetition, so please use this set of instructions as a reminder as required when working through other techniques.

Tools & Materials

- 1 piece of copper sheet, 50mm x 25mm, 0.3mm thick
- Basic tool kit
- Micro-Fold Brake

1. Anneal the piece of copper sheet. Pickle, then clean thoroughly using pumice powder and washing-up liquid to remove any acid traces. Dry thoroughly.

2. Set up the Micro-Fold Brake in a fixed stable position by either screwing it to the bench, clamping it with G-clamps or holding it securely in a vice. Check the metal rollers are clean before using them. A soft brush such as an old toothbrush or paintbrush is ideal for running along the rollers to remove any dust or debris that will leave unsightly marks on the metal.

3. Set the roller thickness appropriate for the thickness of the metal sheet. In this example, using 0.3mm-thick sheet, a quarter turn is about right. Getting a feel for setting the correct thickness will come with practice.

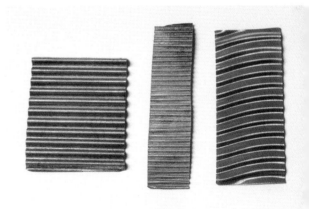

Fig. 4.14 Three corrugated copper samples, from left to right: using the Bonny Doon Micro-Fold Brake, using the Zig Zag machine, using the wavy paper crimper.

4. Work in the middle of the rollers when corrugating sheet metal, and to the sides when corrugating wires. To obtain straight lines in line with the edge of the metal, be very careful when lining it up to the rollers and make sure you have got it in line. Turn the handle with one hand while holding the metal steady with the other and allow it to pass through the rollers.

5. To get even more defined folds, anneal and clean the metal as in step 1, then pass through a second time. If it still isn't defined enough, tighten the rollers and pass the metal through again.

Fig. 4.15 Copper sheet which has been cross-corrugated. The rollers were opened wider for the second pass.

Fig. 4.16 Two partial corrugation samples. The right-hand sample combines both partial corrugation and cross-corrugation by partially corrugating a second time.

Corrugating Textured Surfaces

Texturing the surface of the corrugation prior to corrugation can create some interesting effects. Experiment with applying different textures, for example roll-printed textures from fabric or leaf skeletons, or hammered textures, or a pattern created from striking letter punches on the metal. The more defined or dramatic the pattern, the more clearly it will show up once corrugated.

Cross-corrugation

Running the metal through the corrugator a second time but at a different angle can create wonderful textures, which appear rather like woven cloth. Experiment with different angles and tighter or looser pressure on the rollers. As corrugation work-hardens the metal, it is usually advisable to anneal between each pass. When changing to the second angle, the rollers usually need to be loosened to accommodate the now wider metal from the first round of corrugation.

If you have a wavy crimper, try crimping with this also, and mixing it with the straight rollers.

If you are cross-corrugating a narrow strip, the easiest way to do this is to corrugate by feeding in the widest edge parallel with the rollers first, then the narrow edge second.

Partial Corrugation

An adjustable crimping machine such as the Micro-Fold Brake has the added capacity to partially crimp the metal. To achieve this, simply open the rollers so that the metal can be inserted between them without marking, then, holding the metal in the position where you would like the crimping to begin, tighten the rollers to the appropriate width to begin crimping, ensuring you tighten them equally to create an even pressure across the sheet. Turn the handle slowly so that the number of crimps can be determined, and when you have created as many as you would like, release the metal from the corrugator by loosening the thumbscrews on either side. Make sure you loosen them equally to create a neat finish, and ease them gently out from the rollers to reveal the partial corrugation.

Using Paper

Paper is an incredibly versatile addition when used with annealed metal in a plain rolling mill, and in much the same way it can be used to great effect in corrugation.

For example, use paper cut-outs to create a patterned texture on the corrugated metal. Cut out shapes from paper or cut holes in a sheet of paper, then sandwich between two pieces of annealed copper sheet. Corrugate tightly and then remove the paper to reveal the pattern underneath.

Crimping

Crimping adds a further dimension to corrugation. It transforms a uniform set of ridges into something quite different, which can lead to unique patterns and textures.

Basic Crimping

Tools & Materials

- 1 piece of copper sheet, 50mm x 50mm, 0.5mm thick
- Basic tool kit
- Micro-Fold Brake
- Confirming pliers

Fig. 4.17 Using the Swanstrom Confirming Pliers to crimp the folds.

Fig. 4.18 Two copper samples: the left is before crimping, and the right is after crimping. This shows that after crimping the corrugation reduces in size by at least a third.

1. Anneal and corrugate the copper square.

2. Anneal.

3. Working on a flat surface, starting in one corner, insert the confirming pliers into two troughs either side of a crest until they are pushed down as deep as possible, then gently squeeze together. Work along the rest of the row, overlapping the crimping action slightly to get the smoothest line. Crimping too hard will mark the metal.

4. Repeat for the remaining rows.

Fans and Rosettes

A fan or rosette shape can be easily created from a rectangle that has been corrugated and then crimped.

Tools & Materials
- 1 piece of copper sheet, 80mm x 20mm, 0.5mm thick
- Basic tool kit
- Micro-Fold Brake
- Confirming pliers
- Flat nylon pliers

1. Anneal and corrugate the copper strip, lining the short side up with the rollers. This should result in a reduced overall size of approximately 60mm by 20mm.

2. Anneal again. Now, using the confirming pliers or modified flat-nosed pliers, crimp the crests along one of the long edges. As the metal is crimped, it should start to close together along this edge, causing the strip to start to curve inwards. The wider the crimped section, the more pronounced this will be, but it is best not to take it more than about halfway across the width.

3. Now start to crimp this same edge again, crimping crests together in pairs to bring the curve in even tighter.

4. The curve can stretch further along the outer edge; use nylon pliers to gently ease open the crimping.

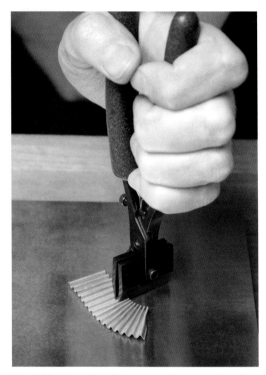

Fig. 4.19 Crimping along one edge to create a fan.

Fig. 4.20 Fan and rosette copper samples.

Fig. 4.21 'Large Rosette Ring' by Emma Turpin featuring a stunning hand-pleated fine silver rosette cluster on a handmade sterling silver ring shank. Rosette measures 40mm in diameter.

Fig. 4.22 'Rosette Cluster Pendant' by Emma Turpin. This hand pleated fine silver cluster rosette pendant measures 4cm in diameter.

By playing around with proportions a semi-circle or fan can be created, or even a complete circle, which looks rather like a ribbon rosette. When a complete circle is made, the centre point creates a natural place to fit a granule or stone setting. Crimping can also be varied and applied in a more irregular way to create more organic-looking shapes.

Corrugated Spiral

A spiral can be created from a tapered strip of metal sheet, crimping along one edge in a similar way to creating a fan.

Fig. 4.23 Finely crafted 'Smoky Quartz Necklace' by Emma Turpin, featuring hand-pleated fine silver rosettes on gold-plated, silver wire detail and faceted smoky quartz beads. Each loop measures 20mm in diameter with 10mm-diameter rosettes.

Fig. 4.24 Finely crafted 'Rosette Loop Drop Earrings' by Emma Turpin, featuring hand pleated fine silver rosettes on gold plated silver wire detail loop and hook fittings. Each earring is approximately 23mm in diameter.

Fig. 4.25 Delicate 'Rosette Studs' created by Emma Turpin. These hand pleated fine silver rosettes on 22ct gold plated backs measure 10mm in diameter.

Spanish Roof Tile Pattern

This pattern looks very like a traditional Mediterranean tiled roof, even more so if made in copper as the warm orange tone is like terracotta tiles.

Tools & Materials

- 1 piece of copper sheet, 50mm x 50mm, 0.3mm thick
- Basic tool kit
- Micro-Fold Brake
- Confirming pliers

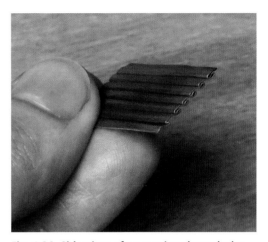

Fig. 4.26 Side view after passing through the rolling mill to flatten the crests.

1. Anneal and corrugate the sheet, perhaps passing through a second time to ensure it is well defined. Anneal again.

2. Using the confirming pliers, gently crimp all the crests.

3. Still using the confirming pliers, gently start to move each crimped crest to one side, so that they all lean in the same direction.

4. Once this has been done across the whole piece, gently mallet down to flatten the metal. Pass it through the rolling mill, exerting only light pressure to flatten.

Fig. 4.27 The resulting Spanish roof tile pattern.

5. Anneal and cross-corrugate to complete the roof pattern.

Finishing Suggestion

If you have used copper or silver for this texture, it could be oxidized then rubbed back to further accentuate the shadows between the pleats.

Smocking

Smocking is a traditional needlework technique largely done by hand for pleating and stitching fabric to create sections that can stretch. It originally evolved as a way to create elasticity in garments prior to the invention of elastic and so was found on cuffs, and across necklines and bodices.

Taking some of the traditional smocking patterns as inspiration, smocking can be recreated in sheet metal to give some very detailed and intricate patterns. There are endless possibilities so this is just one example from which experimentation can begin. The difference with working in metal is that no thread is required. The pleats can be simply squeezed together with pliers and they stay in place, whereas when working in fabric a stitch would be required; this stitch is often made visible as a feature of the needlework.

For a decorative variation, after crimping holes could be drilled in the metal corrugation and wires in the same or a contrasting metal could be threaded through to make the finished item look even more like traditional smocking.

Fig. 4.28 Close-up of smocking detail across the bodice of a baby romper.

Honeycomb Smocking

Honeycomb is a traditional smocking stitch, which can be recreated in metal corrugation. It is also known as the diamond pattern. It can be worked over the whole piece as in this set of instructions, or perhaps just a few rows in much the same way as it would appear on the front of a dress. In this example, the modified round-nosed pliers have been used, but the same technique would work well with flat pliers too.

Tools & Materials
- 1 piece of copper sheet, 50mm x 70mm, 0.3mm thick
- Basic tool kit
- Micro-Fold Brake
- Confirming pliers
- Modified round-nosed pliers
- Ruler
- Fine-tipped marker pen

1. Corrugate the metal sheet, feeding the narrow edge in line with the rollers; the piece should now be roughly square.

2. Anneal, then gently confirm all the crests of the entire piece. The tighter the confirming is at this stage, the more angular the overall smocking will be. Try to keep the rows as even as possible.

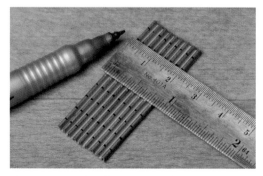

Fig. 4.29 Drawing lines across the crests at 5mm intervals with a steel ruler and a fine marker pen.

Fig. 4.30 Squeezing together crests using customized round-nosed pliers.

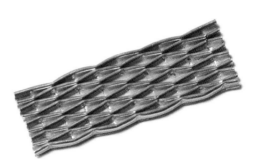

Fig. 4.32 The resulting smocked copper piece.

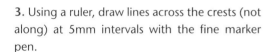

Fig. 4.31 Continuing to work on alternated rows to create smocking across the whole sample.

3. Using a ruler, draw lines across the crests (not along) at 5mm intervals with the fine marker pen.

4. Using the modified round-nosed pliers, squeeze together every other pair of confirmed crests along the first and second rows.

5. Now squeeze together the markings left out in the previous row, this time squeezing rows two and three together.

6. Continue working alternate rows until the smocking is complete over the whole piece.

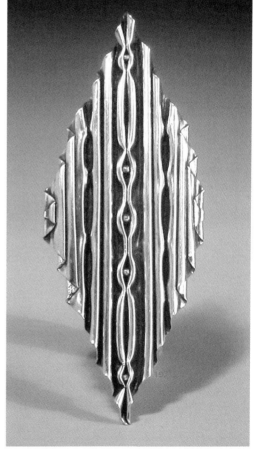

Fig. 4.33 'Sampler Brooch' by Cynthia Eid in silver with gold granules, showing several techniques including crimping, smocking (front and back) and granulation.

Fig. 4.34 Folding the metal in half with paper trapped inside.

Fig. 4.35 Leaf after corrugating before opening.

Fold Forming and Corrugation

Fold forming and corrugation combined together create some very interesting outcomes.

The metal can become very tightly pressed together and so is very difficult to open. A way to combat this is to insert a soft material such as paper between the two layers to allow a little space to insert the fine tip of a burnisher or watch-back opening tool. (*See* Chapter 2 for advice on opening out folded forms.)

How to Make a Corrugated Folded Leaf

These lovely leaves remind me of beech leaves and work particularly well in copper, which can be heated with a torch to create some wonderful colours on the surface of the metal. Be particularly careful when opening the leaves out as the edges can be very sharp (*see* Chapter 1 for guidance on appropriate safety measures).

Tools & Materials

- 1 piece of copper sheet, 80mm x 40mm, 0.3mm thick
- Basic tool kit
- Micro-Fold Brake
- Fine-edged burnisher or similar fold forming opening tool

1. Anneal the metal sheet. Fold in half along the length; if working in metal which is 0.3mm thick, it will be possible to bend it with your fingers. The folded metal should now measure approximately 80mm by 20mm. Tuck a piece of thick paper inside the fold.

2. Compress the fold gently by malleting the fold on a steel flat plate.

Fig. 4.36 The resulting leaf once opened.

3. Corrugate; this looks most leaf-like if done on a slight angle.

4. Anneal, taking extra care as the piece of paper will burn out. Insert the fine tip of the burnisher to start opening the fold, then when it is open enough to get hold of the edges with your fingers, continue to open out by hand and the corrugated leaf is revealed.

RIGHT: **Fig. 4.37 'Dew Edged Earrings' by Cynthia Eid in Argentium silver.**

Repoussé And Corrugation

Working into a piece of metal corrugation using the technique of repoussé can produce some very interesting results.

Tools & Materials

- 1 piece of copper sheet, 0.3–0.5mm thick
- Basic tool kit
- Any corrugation tool
- Bowl of pitch
- Chasing or repoussé punches, or steel doming punches
- Chasing hammer

1. Anneal and corrugate the piece of copper sheet.

2. Anneal.

Fig. 4.38 Creating repoussé patterns by striking a doming punch with a chasing hammer while the copper is supported in a bowl of pitch.

3. Gently warm the bowl of pitch with a soft flame and when it starts to become the consistency of syrup, place the corrugation in place. Allow the pitch to cool a little until it holds its shape but has some give.

4. Select your repoussé tool and gradually begin to work into the corrugation by striking the punches with the chasing hammer to create the pattern you would like. As the metal work-hardens, remove by gently warming the pitch again with a soft flame and lift out with steel tweezers. Anneal and pickle before returning to the pitch again. Both sides of the metal can be worked to create your chosen design.

Wire Corrugation

Corrugating wire lengths is quick and easy, and so is ideal to use in creating batch production pieces such as matching necklace links. Starting with round wire is ideal, as the rounded shape means there are no sharp edges on the corrugation, which is one of the drawbacks of working in sheet metal.

Making Corrugated Wire Chain Links

These simple corrugated chain links could be incorporated into a longer chain or used individually as drop earrings by adding an ear hook.

Tools & Materials

- 1 piece of round silver wire, 0.8mm; for a 2cm diameter link you will need approx. 9cm of wire
- Basic tool kit
- Micro-Fold Brake

**Fig. 4.39
Silver corrugated
wire links.**

1. Anneal the wire. Ensure it is rinsed well and thoroughly dried after pickling.

2. Brush along the rollers with a soft brush to ensure it is dust-free.

3. Pass the wire through the brake close to one of the sides. Always do this with wire, as it puts more isolated pressure on the rollers and is therefore more likely to mark them. If you are happy with the corrugated effect, continue to the next step. If you would prefer a more defined corrugation, tighten the rollers slightly then pass the wire through a second time.

4. File the ends flat, then gently ease them round to meet. Solder the joint closed, pickle and dry.

5. Tap the link very gently on a tapered ring mandrel supported in a vice to round the shape of the link, without losing the definition of the corrugation. Incorporate the link into your design as required, and finish by polishing in a barrel polisher.

Variations

A piece of wire could be rolled flat first in a conventional rolling machine before corrugation for a further variation.

Once the link has been created, each crest of the corrugation can be crimped closed with crimping pliers to create a more star-like shape.

Fine wires can be corrugated for use in the enamelling technique cloisonné.

Layering Corrugation

Layering corrugation is best done with metals of the same thickness to get a perfect join for soldering. If the work needs to remain work-hard, pieces can also be joined using cold connections, for example rivets.

Corrugating a piece of wire to solder along the edge of a piece of corrugation may be a useful way to overcome the sharp edge of the thin material.

Fig. 4.40 Starting to bring the two edges together.

Fig. 4.41 Starting to crimp the end of the bead with customized flat pliers.

Fig. 4.42 How the end of the bead should look after all the crests have been crimped.

Making Corrugated Beads

These beads feel very rigid and strong, and are wonderfully tactile.

Tools & Materials

- 1 piece of copper sheet, 60mm x 40mm, 0.4mm thick
- Basic tool kit
- Micro-Fold Brake
- Confirming pliers

1. Anneal and corrugate the piece of metal, lining up the shorter edge with the rollers, resulting in a sheet that is roughly square once corrugated.

2. Gently wrap the corrugation around a tapered mandrel until the two edges overlap slightly. Take care not to squash or distort the corrugation.

3. Solder the edge. To do this, pull the two edges slightly apart and flux both edges generously where they overlap. Place a series of small pieces of solder (paillons) all along one side of the join. Heat until these have just melted. Apply more flux to both sides and then overlap the joint again and hold in place at either end with reverse action tweezers; heat again to melt the solder and form the join. Pickle, rinse and dry thoroughly.

4. Gently push the corrugated cylinder onto the mandrel again to true up as it may have become distorted during soldering. Turn over and repeat with the other end.

5. Now working at one end of the cylinder, start to confirm the folds, pushing the metal inwards as you do. Work around one end and then the other.

6. Place in a vice and very gently turn the handle to start closing the vice. The bead should compress further and the centre will begin to

Fig. 4.43 Hold in a vice and turn the handle very slowly to force the middle of the bead to bulge out.

Fig. 4.44 The finished copper bead after brass wire brushing.

bulge out. Take it as far as you feel you would like to.If the bead is not completely square this may create quite a distorted shape; part of the bead could even start to concave inwards.

7. File the ends to soften, then finished as desired.

Variations

Partially cross-corrugate the metal before forming the cylinder. This will make it more difficult to line up the edges to solder the seam.

Add interest to the end of the beads by soldering on an end cap, which could be made from either a flat or a domed disc of sheet metal.

Make simpler flat-sided beads from a narrow strip formed into a cylinder, by soldering flat discs cut from 0.5mm or thicker silver sheet, with holes drilled in the centre onto either end of the cylinder.

Fig. 4.45 'Talisher' by Cynthia Eid, featuring three beautiful corrugated silver beads.

DEVELOPMENT AND DESIGN RESOLUTION

This chapter introduces a few unusual fold-forming techniques that do not quite fit into the other categories in this book, as well as ideas for techniques to complement fold forming and some guidance on resolving designs into functional pieces.

The wide range of fold-forming techniques introduced in this book aims to inspire, but ultimately it will be the individual reader's interpretation, experimentation and development of these techniques that will lead to the most original and exciting outcomes. To enable and encourage this journey, this chapter provides some pointers for possible further avenues of research. There are many possibilities but I've laid out a few ideas and hope that the suggestions will help to spark other creative thoughts or combinations of techniques that might produce interesting results. The ideas are still largely based on using the basic jewellery-making tools described in Chapter 1. As a small aside, it is worth mentioning that several fold formers have done some very interesting research using the hydraulic press, which is not included in this book; as a tool it has great possibilities for fold forming.

Unusual Fold-Forming Techniques

Belly Button Fold

This technique is quick and effective and easy to repeat multiple times in a piece of sheet metal. As a dome is formed in the middle of a flat sheet of metal, I suggest using wood as the supporting material underneath the metal while the dome is formed. Using the end grain is most effective as it will give more easily as it is struck. Softwoods such as pine work very well as due to their softness they will not mark the metal surface. Using a steel or brass doming block to support the metal underneath would result in the edges of the domes marking lines into the metal as the dome is formed. Other soft materials such as a leather sandbag or piece of rubber can be used in place of the wood.

Tools & Materials

- 1 copper sheet, 50mm x 50mm, roughly 0.3mm thick
- Basic tool kit
- Steel doming punches
- Softwood offcut

1. Anneal, pickle, rinse and dry the copper sheet.

2. Support the metal sheet on the end grain of an offcut of wood; the wood can be supported

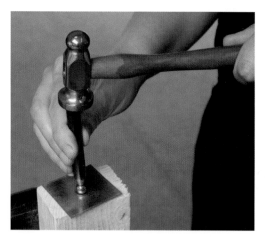

Fig. 5.1 Creating a dome in the centre of a piece of annealed copper sheet using a doming punch struck with a chasing hammer, supporting the copper on the end grain of a softwood offcut held in a vice.

Fig. 5.2 The dome created in the middle of the sheet of copper.

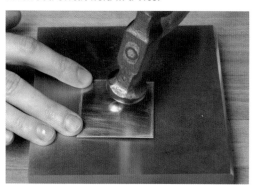

Fig. 5.3 Using the curved face of a planishing hammer to compress the top of the dome, forcing it downwards.

Fig. 5.4 The resulting belly button fold.

Fig. 5.5 The belly button fold can be repeated using different-sized doming punches across a sheet of metal.

in a vice for stability if required. Strike the doming punch with an old engineer's hammer or a chasing punch to create a dome in the middle of the sheet of metal.

3. Turn the metal over, and now, resting on a flat steel plate or anvil, strike the dome quite hard with the curved face of a planishing hammer. The top of the dome will collapse but the edge of the dome remains raised. Turn the metal over to view the resulting belly button fold. To understand what has happened in this process, it is worth explaining how the metal has been work-

hardened. When the doming punch is forced by the strike of the hammer down into the sheet metal, the metal stretches and hardens. The edge of the dome is where the metal stretches, yet the top of the dome remains relatively soft as this part has simply moved because the metal around it has stretched. So the edge of the dome is work-hardened and the centre of the dome is still annealed. This allows the top part of the dome to collapse as it is struck with the planishing hammer, while the edge of the fold does not move because it is harder.

Interlocking Folds

A further progression from creating multiple folds in a single piece of metal is to interlock and fold form separate pieces of metal to create multiple folded pieces. Inspiration for these could come from crafts such as origami, weaving and basketry. These fold-formed pieces can include simple planished folds as described in the folded 'paper' chain below, or become more complex and dynamic by forging along open edges or folded edges.

Folded 'Paper' Chain

This techniques involves interlocking two long narrow strips, and will probably be familiar as a paper chain-making technique. In paper it is often made in two contrasting colours, so likewise in metal this would be effective in two contrasting metals, for example in copper and silver.

For a very narrow, intricate folded chain, try rolling down some wire to make a flat strip. This has the added benefit of being very even in width as well as giving nice rounded sides, meaning there are no sharp edges in the final concertina form.

Tools & Materials

- 2 pieces of metal sheet, 120mm x 6mm, roughly 0.3mm thick
- Basic tool kit

1. Solder the two strips of metal together at one end, at right angles to each other, as pictured in Fig. 5.6. While using the blow torch during soldering, anneal all the metal.

2. Pickle, rinse and dry after soldering and annealing.

3. Fold the one strip (then the one underneath) over the other and planish along the fold to confirm the fold.

Fig. 5.6 The two strips of copper have been soldered together at right angles.

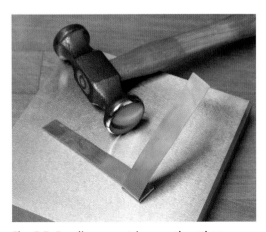

Fig. 5.7 Bending one strip over the other.

4. Now fold the second strip over the first strip and planish along the fold.

5. Keep repeating steps 3 and 4 until you reach the end of the metal strips.

6. Solder the other ends together as before. This will also anneal the metal ready for opening.

7. Gently open out your interlocking chain, to reveal the woven concertina pattern.

Fig. 5.8 Compressing the fold by striking with a planishing hammer supported on a steel flat plate.

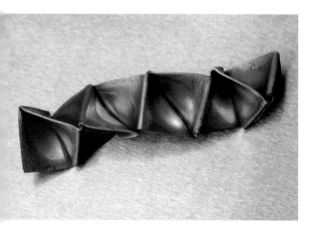

Fig. 5.9 The resulting interlocking chain once it has been opened out.

Alternative Approaches to Fold-Forming Techniques

A Different Starting Point

Many of the techniques in this book start with flat sheet metal. Consider using wire or tube in different profiles and applying fold-forming techniques to them. For example, to create a tight bend in round wire, anneal, fold, compress with a planishing hammer, anneal and open again. This is far quicker than soldering, and the result is stronger too.

Fig. 5.10 Using a planishing hammer to confirm a fold in a piece of annealed copper wire.

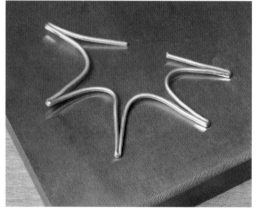

Fig. 5.11 Five confirmed folds at intervals along a strip of round copper wire.

Fig. 5.12 After annealing, the folded wire can be opened out, leaving a tight and strong bend in the wire.

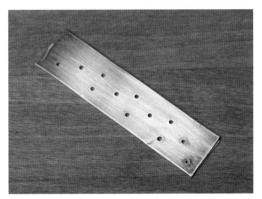

Fig. 5.13 Holes have been drilled in this piece of copper while it is folded up.

Drilling

Experiment with drilling holes in pieces while they are folded up. This will result in a symmetrical pattern with the line of the fold as the centre of the symmetry when the piece is opened out after fold forming. Perhaps try on some multiple folded pieces; for example, the Heistad cup in Chapter 3 could be very interesting as the holes would distort as the piece is rolled.

Fig. 5.14 The fold has been opened out to reveal the symmetrical pattern of drilled holes.

Rolling Mill Textures

Use other materials to add texture when using the rolling mill to confirm folds. Effective materials for texturing include cut-out paper shapes, fabric, ribbons and leaf skeletons. With materials containing water, such as fresh plant material, make sure you create a sandwich with a piece of scrap metal such as some brass sheet so that the plant material does not come into contact with the steel metal rollers, as this could cause rust on the surface of the rollers.

RIGHT: Fig. 5.15
Fold-formed leaf pendant in sterling silver by Louise Mary Muttitt, where a leaf skeleton was passed through the rolling mill to create the leaf vein texture on the inside of the leaf.

Fig. 5.16 Earrings by Megan Arnold, Argentium silver and 22ct yellow gold. The granules are located in the grooves of the micro corrugation. The properties of Argentium silver mean it is ideal for metal corrugation and fusing.

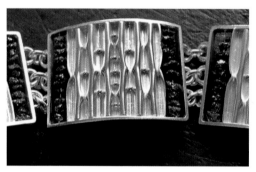

Fig. 5.17 Bracelet detail by Megan Arnold, Argentium silver, 22ct yellow gold and rough-cut diamonds. This illustrates how smocking creates ideal pockets for granulation. In this piece Megan has used the underside of the smocking as the front.

Granulation

Add granulation to enhance fold-formed pieces. Granulation can be particularly effective in corrugation, particularly smocking, as this naturally has ideal pockets to locate the granules.

Fig. 5.18 'Fold-Formed Beads Bracelet' by Charles Lewton-Brain. In this bracelet, the forged folds have become the setting to hold the beads in place.

Gemstones

Consider ways to incorporate gemstones into a fold-formed piece for a contrasting colour and texture. For example, a simple rub-over bezel stone setting could be enhanced with the addition of a piece of corrugated wire as a decorative edge around the bezel.

Enamelling

Enamelling suits fold forming very well. Many fold-formed pieces can be created without soldering and as such high temperatures are required for enamelling, this means they are ideal starting forms to enamel onto. Enamel can also strengthen very thin corrugated copper sheet, making it more practical for use in functional items such as jewellery. A specialist enamelling kiln is not required for enamelling; it is possible to do basic enamelling using a blow torch.

Resolving Designs

Inspiration

Gathered visual research is a useful resource to help resolve designs. Some designs can begin from a piece of visual research, interpreted through fold-forming techniques; others might start from a successful fold-forming experiment.

Areas to look for inspiration for fold forming include:

- nature – in particular leaves and shells
- engineering
- architecture
- textiles and fashion

One of the more challenging aspects of jewellery and silverware design is resolving a design concept or successful experiment into a functional piece. The resolution of designs from early copper experiments to final wearable, functional or sculptural pieces is vital to their success. At the beginning of the process, decide which aspect is the strongest feature of the design; keep this in mind and use this decision to inform your choices as the piece resolves, so that the piece does not become too diluted from what originally made it distinctive.

There are many elements to consider when resolving a design. Below are listed some of the key ones, with particular references to fold forming. Each element can be directly affected by another; the aim is to have all of them working together in the piece effectively.

Fig. 5.19 'Twist Candlesticks' in Britannia silver by Louise Mary Muttitt.

Fig. 5.20 'Folded Leaf Vase' in sterling silver by Louise Mary Muttitt.

Fig. 5.21 'Con Brio' by Theresa Nguyen, Britannia silver, 30cm tall by 57cm wide. 'Con Brio' explores the concept of energy in a form, capturing a sense of organic movement and the vitality of creation.

Function

Finished pieces will have a function that will need to be considered at the resolution stage. Even sculptural pieces will have some parameters which will need to be considered at the design stage, such as size or budget for materials.

Sculptures

Amongst the considerations here are the audience or client, scale, whether it is an indoor or outdoor sculpture, stability, practicalities of manufacture, and the message it conveys in the style.

Functional Pieces

Considerations can be wide-ranging: from ergonomics, such as how comfortable a spoon is to hold, to how well a jug pours, durability, and stability for vessels such as vases. Thicker gauges of metal may be required to help with durability. Fold forming can be carried out on thicker metals; the thicker the metal, however, the harder it is to re-open the form after fold forming. I have successfully fold formed 1.1mm-thick sterling silver sheet on many occasions and have found it to be a good thickness for silverware items.

DESIGN DEVELOPMENT CASE STUDY: CROSS BROOCH

This sterling silver cross brooch was a private commission for a client who wanted to mark the occasion of being ordained. She approached me to create a cross for her, having seen my silver leaf spoons in an exhibition, and specified that she would like me to create a piece that followed the same design aesthetic. In addition, she wanted the piece to function both as a brooch and a pendant.

After receiving the brief, I did some quick sketches, then used paper models to work out the size and rough proportions of the cross. To develop the three-dimensional elements of the cross, a model was made in a piece of 0.5mm thick copper sheet. After creating a line fold in the sheet metal, the cross shape was cut out before opening the fold, so it would be perfectly symmetrical. Once the first fold, which ran from the top to the bottom of the cross, was opened, I decided that the folded edge should feature on the front of the brooch, as this gave a more solid feel to the piece. It also gave a neat place on the reverse to insert a pendant loop. The cross 'arms' were then shaped with soft mallets

Fig. 5.22 The original leaf spoon design by Louise Mary, made from sterling silver and featuring a single line fold.

over curved metal formers after fold forming. I contemplated adding a horizontal fold but decided that I preferred the simpler effect of a single fold.

The resulting cross retains the leaf like quality of the original leaf spoons, while also being a distinctive representation of the symbol of a cross, and functions as both a brooch and a pendant.

Fig. 5.23 The final cross brooch in sterling silver incorporates the line fold and tapered points at the top and bottom much like the leaf spoon.

Fig. 5.24 In addition to the brooch pin, a loop at the top of the cross on the reverse side allows it to also be hung from a chain and worn as a pendant.

Jewellery

Consider how wearable the piece is: is it a one-off catwalk piece or an everyday item? Practicalities will include sizing for bracelets, rings and necklaces (these may well be bespoke to the client). Trying on metal experiments can help resolve practical issues such as weight, fit and how it hangs if it is a necklace or earring. Many jewellery pieces will need findings, for example ear hooks or ear wires for earrings; aim to integrate the findings as fluidly as possible into the design.

Metal Choice

Metal choice will depend largely on intended function and budget. Base metals are generally not suitable for pieces that come into contact with skin unless they are protected with a lacquer or similar. Other considerations may include whether the metal is food-safe, or if it will be exposed to elements and the resulting effect over time, for example acid rain on a garden sculpture. When selecting a metal, be aware that different metals have different work-hardness properties. Copper is one of the more malleable metals, so when transferring a design from a copper experiment into another metal

Fig. 5.25 'Parissa' by Theresa Nguyen, Britannia silver, 85cm wide by 21cm tall. Theresa's design ideas were initially developed into models made from the leaves of a *Camellia Japonica*. This silver centrepiece reflects growth and begins with small units resembling leaf forms and then multiples to form a complete whole.

Fig. 5.26 'Persephone' vase by Rauni Higson, made from Britannia silver, 55cm tall. This piece demonstrates a beautiful integration of fold formed elements with chased and raised pieces to create a cohesive overall design, with very strong references to nature.

such as sterling silver, remember that the piece will probably work-harden more quickly so will need to be annealed more frequently.

When creating a T-fold, for example, part of the original sheet is cut away after forming. If using precious metals, making a mixed metal sheet by using a base metal such as copper for the part that will be cut away saves using such a large piece of precious material.

Bi-metal

Bi-metal is available from the USA and is silver with a layer of gold pressure bonded together, to create a material in which the gold layer is durable enough to form an even texture without revealing the silver underneath. This contrast can look very effective when used in dynamic fold-formed pieces.

Scale

Scale can be a restriction. Consider the application of the piece carefully when deciding on the size of the design. Large often has great impact; however, sometimes miniature can have its own impressive appeal. Size may also by restricted by the size of your equipment, for example the width of a rolling mill. Repeating units can be a way to increase scale, by making several smaller, more manageable pieces.

Folds and Edges

Most fold-formed pieces will include these two main elements. Edges in particular can be very thin and sharp. For functional items such as jewellery they will at the very least need to be filed and polished to soften them. It may also be possible to fold over the edges. In corrugation this can be done before corrugating, giving a rounded edge with the added benefit of extra strength from the double thickness.

Another metalworking method used to thicken and strengthen edges is caulking. Use a creasing or raising hammer at 90° to the edge to strike overlapping blows down onto this edge. This will create a hammered texture and produces a slightly thicker edge. In silversmithing this is traditionally done around the top of vessels during raising. Ideally, support the work on a sandbag while caulking.

Striking a series of overlapping hammer blows with a raising or creasing hammer onto the folded edge will result in a decorative hammered texture along the fold.

Cutting patterns along edges of fold-formed pieces would add a decorative element. If this is done while a piece is still folded, the resulting edges will be symmetrical once opened. Be aware that if you cut into a folded edge at any point it will considerably weaken the structure of the final form at that point.

Finish

When selecting a finish the practicalities of the use of the design will be an important consideration, as surface finishes can wear off or get scratched over time on pieces that are used as tableware and jewellery. As well as practical considerations, make use of the form and textures within the piece and highlight these aspects through surface finish choices.

Simple finishes can be very effective. Matt finishes tend to show off the form more clearly, as reflections in a polished surface can be distracting. A simple burnished edge can add interest in the form of a highlight. Partially patinating a piece can be effective too; it especially works well in the texture of metal corrugation, where it can be rubbed away from the raised surfaces and remains dark in the recesses. Patinated surfaces usually need protecting from wear with a lacquer or beeswax polish.

APPENDIX

Suppliers

UK Suppliers

Argex Ltd
130 Hockley Hill, Hockley, Birmingham, B18 5AN
Tel: +44 121 248 4344
Web: www.argex.co.uk
silver bullion (wide range of sheet, wire, tube, solder)

Bellore Rashbel
39 Greville Street, London, EC1N 8PJ
Tel: +44 207 4043 220
Web: www.bellore.org.uk
silver and gold bullion, findings, chain

Betts Metal Sales
49–63 Spencer Street, Hockley,
Birmingham, B18 6DE
Tel: +44 121 233 2413
Web: www.bettsmetalsales.com
silver and gold bullion, Argentium silver, findings, jewellery and metalsmithing tools, refining service for scrap silver

Cookson Precious Metals Ltd
59–83 Vittoria Street, Birmingham, B1 3NZ
Tel: +44 121 200 2120
Web: www.cooksongold.com
silver and gold bullion, findings and beads, jewellery and metalsmithing tools, refining service for scrap silver

John Keatley (Metals) Ltd,
33–35 Shadwell Street, Birmingham, B4 6HD
Tel: +44 121 236 4300
Web: www.johnkeatleymetals.com
copper, brass, steel, for samples and toolmaking, sheet metal cut to required dimensions, counter service has low cost sheet metal offcuts ideal for experiments

Marcia Lanyon
P.O. Box 370, London, W6 7NJ
Tel: +44 207 602 2446
Web: www.marcialanyon.co.uk
gemstones, pearls, beads

Presman Mastermelt
56 Hatton Garden, London, EC1N 8HP
Tel: 0207 400 3400
Web: www.mastermeltgroup.com
Email: info@mastermelts.co.uk scrap@presman.co.uk
trusted by the industry for over 70 years for scrap buying and precious metal recovery from jewellery workshop waste

HS Walsh & Sons Ltd
Hunter House, Biggin Hill Airport, Churchill Way, Biggin Hill, Kent, TN16 3BN
Tel: +44 1959 543660
Web: www.hswalsh.com
jewellery and metalsmithing tools

International Suppliers

Gill Mechanical Company
P.O. Box 24628, Eugene, OR 97402, USA
Web: www.tubewringer.com
Email: info@tubewringer.com
manufacturers and suppliers of tube wringers used to corrugate sheet metal

Otto Frei
126 2nd Street, Oakland, CA 94607, USA
Web: www.ottofrei.com
supplier of large and small corrugating mills

Rio Grande
7500 Bluewater Rd NW, Albuquerque,
NM 87121, USA
Web: www.riogrande.com
supplier of microfolding tools: Bonny Doon
Micro-Fold Brake, Swanstrom confirming pliers;
also sheet bi-metal made from 22ct gold pressure
bonded to Argentium silver; worldwide delivery
available

Profiform
See website for list of distributors
Web: www.profiform.com
Profiform Proco (a metal corrugation machine
similar to the Bonny Doon Micro-Fold Brake)

Fold-forming Resources

Artists Directory

The artists listed here have kindly provided photographs of their work for this book, which have illus-
trated the diverse range of possibilities of fold forming.

Megan Arnold

meganarnold.weebly.com
Megan likes to work
with all gold and silver,
including Argentium.
She likes exploring many
varied and ancient tech-

niques, developing ideas from the process of the
technique itself along with natural forms. Fluidity is a
constant in all her work, ensuring that all pieces move
well, reflecting and catching light on the surfaces of
the metal, but at the same time being comfortable
to wear. Megan particularly enjoys the possibilities
of metal corrugation, creating very different textures and surfaces for the light to reflect on. Megan
began making jewellery in 1998 training with the
renowned jeweller Yehudit Shorr at the De Cordova
School in Lincoln, Massachusetts, USA. After her
return to the UK in 2001, she established a home
studio in rural Herefordshire, with relatively easy
access to Birmingham's historic Jewellery Quarter.

Cynthia Eid

www.cynthiaeid.com
Whether using hammers or
hydraulic press tools, Cynthia Eid's
work shows her fascination with
the paradox that a soft, fluid-look-
ing metal form can evolve from a
flat, stiff rectangle. The forms she makes have their
roots in walks through her gardens, the woods and
along the water's edge. The similarities to nature
occur through her sense of beauty and observa-
tions as she moves the metal, gathering inspiration
through process and serendipity. After beginning
with a basic plan, the metal and she have a conversa-
tion as the form is resolved. She has been entranced
by the immediacy of fold forming since 1996, lov-
ing the surprise moment when opening a fold
form. Since 1999, Cynthia has worked primarily in
Argentium silver, appreciating its fire stain free mal-
leability, fusing, granulation, and tarnish resistance.
Starting at fourteen years of age, Cynthia Eid has
worked metal for fifty years. With degrees in Art
Education and Jewellery, Design, and Silversmithing, she has also worked as a bench jeweller for fine
goldsmiths and model-maker in a gold jewellery
factory. Her work is in museums in the US and UK.
Currently an independent metalsmith and educa-
tor, she teaches at Metalwerx in Massachusetts, and
has taught in the US, Canada, Europe and Australia.

Rauni Higson

www.raunihigson.co.uk

Rauni Higson creates distinctive, sculptural silverware and jewellery in Snowdonia, North Wales, where she set up her studio in 1997. Movement, flow and growth patterns are a particular preoccupation, as she strives to capture something of the beauty of nature, without directly imitating it. The mountains and coastline of the area are an endless source of inspiration. Working primarily in silver, from small scale jewellery to large scale sculptural tableware, with a wide range of traditional silversmithing and jewellery techniques, finding her own interpretation, or combining techniques to create original design solutions, imbued with the richness of hand skills. Half Finnish, but raised in the UK, she took the opportunity to study in Finland at Lahti Design Institute. She discovered fold-forming on a course with Brian Clarke in Ireland in 2000, and has enjoyed the magic of the process ever since.

Charles Lewton-Brain

www.brainpress.com

Charles Lewton-Brain began his interest in jewellery at the age of seventeen, visiting a Native American named Sonny Spruce in Taos, New Mexico, then went to Art College in Nova Scotia and went on from there. He is based in Canada, but his work has taken him worldwide. Charles works in all metals, and other materials. Process and the nature of the material inspire him. He also gives himself parameters for a piece, structures to work against as a work is planned. His work is about drawing, about mark making with material and about the tension between nature and structure. Allowing the materials to do the work, letting nature show in the work lends it a beauty that he cannot easily reach by forcing form onto the material. The marks of process are compositional elements. This is seen in fold forming work. He has used most types of fold forming in his work, with scoring and bending being primary for a number of years. His work and writing on the results of his technical research have been published internationally. In 1994 Brain Press was established which documents, publishes and markets the results of his research activities.

Louise Mary Muttitt

www.louisemarydesigns.co.uk

Louise has always been drawn towards nature as a source of inspiration for her silversmithing. Through experimentation with creating leaf forms in metal, Louise serendipitously discovered the process of fold forming during the final year of her degree at Sheffield Hallam University in 2005. Louise initially used fold forming as a solution in a design for spoons, but it soon became a technique that she found had a diverse range of applications from small scale jewellery designs through to larger scale functional silverware items such as candelabra. She particularly likes the way that fold forming strengthens sheet metal, and that as it is such an intuitive process, the forms that grow from the metal imitate nature very closely. Much of her work has used the rolling mill to create clean, controlled line folds, which have been used as the main feature of her simple, organic and carefully considered designs. More recent pieces have begun to feature the addition of surface textures to these pieces and she is also working to incorporate more forged folds into her designs.

Theresa Ngyuyen

www.theresanguyen.co.uk

Theresa's workshop is based in Birmingham's famous Jewellery Quarter. She is internationally known for her ability to fashion metals into works of exquisite beauty, craftsmanship and design. Theresa created her first commission, a silver cocktail shaker set, as a result of winning the national Young Designer Silversmith Award in 2005 when she was only nineteen. She is passionate about working closely with her clients in order to design and hand craft unique commissions of decorative art work, silverware or jewellery that will both delight and enable her clients to mark special moments in their lives, give precious gifts to their loved ones and enrich spaces that they live or work in. Meticulous attention to detail at every stage of the process and traditional silversmithing techniques are at the heart of Theresa's work, to create breath-taking moments of joy and treasure that inspire. Theresa hopes to capture the sense of wonder about the world around her in her work. She uses the fold forming technique to convey organic forms and sensuous surfaces. A number of Theresa's pieces form part of prestigious public and private collections and can be viewed at the National Museum of Wales, Cardiff, The Clothworkers' Company and New College, Oxford.

Emma-Jane Rule

www.emma-janerulesilversmith.co.uk

Using the technique of fold forming alongside more traditional metalworking practices such as hammer forming  and hand raising, Emma-Jane Rule explores the malleable and intriguing natures of silver and copper. Encouraging pleated metal to curve and stretch in a designed direction, using hammers or a rolling mill, is a serendipitous way of working that creates many opportunities for the metal to evolve and dictate the final form. Overcoming these challenges and learning how metals move suits Emma's playful and intuitive approach to metalworking. It has underpinned her practice since being introduced to fold forming on the Foundation in Art and Design and then graduating as a mature student in 2015 from De Montfort University, Leicester, with a First Class BA (Hons) Design Crafts. Her work is organic and tactile, reflecting the undulating lines and rhythms found in the natural world, which is where she finds her inspiration. Additional surface textures, patinas and burnishing complement and enhance the forms and the natural lustre of metal. Emma-Jane's designs include jewellery as well as sculptural decorative and functional contemporary silverware and metalwork, unique items of luxury for everyday use and treasured heirlooms for the future.

Emma Turpin

www.emmaturpin.com

Emma Turpin set up her jewellery business after graduating from Middlesex University in 2005, and currently designs and creates her handmade jewellery from her rural workshop based in the Essex countryside. She draws many ideas for her work from traditional crafts and interprets them with her own style. Emma particularly enjoys creating wearable jewellery inspired by the Victorian era, and her love for shapes and patterns is also evident in her work. Her 'Maiden's Garlands' collection is inspired by traditional paper folding and fabric ruffles. Emma developed her micro folding technique while at university, where she had the opportunity to experiment with several materials, including fine silver, which she uses to make her micro folded rosettes. Emma has developed her rosettes using a range of finishes, including oxidization, 22ct gold plating and rose gold plating, and adding striking contrasting details using other components such as semi precious gemstone beads. Emma is continually developing her techniques and her rosettes, from small, detailed rosettes to larger scale singular rosettes worn as single pendants. Due to each one being handmade, no two rosettes are ever the same.

Websites

www.foldforming.org
This is the 'Foldforming Hub', international home of the annual Lewton-Brain Foldform Competition and learning resources for metal artists

www.ganoksin.com
Information resource for jewellers. Ganoksin maintains a substantial library of articles, publications, reports, and technical data on jewellery topics

www.metalcorrugation.com
Website of the metal corrugation specialist, Trish McAleer, including information on her book, *Metal Corrugation*

Books

Creative Metal Forming, Betty Helen Longhi and Cynthia Eid (Brynmorgen Press, 2013).

Fold Forming, Charles Lewton-Brain (Brynmorgen Press, 2008).

Metals Technic, edited by Tim McCreight (Brynmorgen Press, 1992).

Metal Corrugation, Patricia McAleer (Out of the Blue Studio, 2002).

INDEX